# ISRAEL

*God's Covenant People,
God's Promised Land*

## Graham Coates

Copyright © 2018 by Graham Coates
All rights reserved. No part of this book may be reproduced, scanned,
or distributed in any printed or electronic form without permission.
First Edition: December 2018
Printed in the United States of America
ISBN: 1642542229
ISBN: 9781642542226

# CONTENTS

Dedication
Preface
Acknowledgments

### SECTION 1
*God's Covenant People*

Chapter 1  Hosea: Why Care about Israel?
Chapter 2  Genesis—It All Started with Abraham
Chapter 3  The Heresy of Replacement Theology
Chapter 4  Esther—Anti-Semitism

### SECTION 2
*The Bones are Rattling*
*(Israel's Homecoming)*

Chapter 5  The Birth of a Nation
Chapter 6  Ezekiel—A Nation of Dry Bones
Chapter 7  Zechariah—The (Not So) Lost Tribes of Israel
Chapter 8  Joel—Israel, an Undivided Nation

### SECTION 3
Tendons, Flesh, and Skin
(Israel's Development)

Chapter 9   Ezekiel—Tendons (Israel's Resilience)
Chapter 10  Ezekiel—Flesh (Israel's Muscle)
Chapter 11  Ezekiel—Skin (Israel's Beautiful Land)
Chapter 12  Genesis—Blessed to Be a Blessing
Chapter 13  Romans—Israel's Glorious Future

# **DEDICATION**

This book is dedicated to people everywhere who love Israel and seek the truth to be written and spoken about her.

I dedicate this book to everyone who stands with United with Israel.

# PREFACE

*[H]e who touches Israel touches the apple of His eye.*

—Zechariah 2:8

American Preacher Derek Prince was once asked, "Why care about Israel?" A good question, and his answer was as simple as it was profound: "Because God cares about Israel!" Zechariah tells us that Israel is the "Apple of God's eye." Why love Israel? The answer is simple: because God loves Israel.

> Blessed be the Lord your God, who delighted in you [Solomon], setting you on the throne of Israel! Because the Lord has loved Israel forever, therefore He made you king, to do justice and righteousness. (1 Kings 10:9)

In an increasingly crazy world, there is one unfortunate constant: the universal hatred of the Jews. Threats against Israel from ISIS, Hamas, and Hezbollah continue unchecked and unabated. From Iran's Mahmoud Ahmadinejad's[1] cries to destroy Israel to Recep Erdoğan's[2] praise of Adolf Hitler's governance, in addition to Palestinian terrorists, suicide bombers, and countless UN resolutions condemning Israel and supporting her sworn enemies. Everything that God loves, the devil hates! It is no surprise that the devil is passionate about the hatred of Israel.

It is sad enough that the world has always hated the Jews, but even sadder is that this hatred found its way into the church and is justified in an insidious teaching called Replacement Theology.

One reason for this book is my journey of discovery which led to a response to that teaching. Replacement Theology teaches that the church has replaced Israel in God's plan. It argues that the Jews are no longer God's chosen people and God does not have a future plan for the nation of Israel.

As a believer in the God of Abraham, Isaac, and Jacob, and as a believer in Jesus Christ, I cannot help but believe that God desires to bring revelation to us from His Word. I like to call those times "a-ha" moments. My journey of discovery about Israel and God's love for her started in 2012, following one such "a-ha" moment.

This moment came when I was talking to a pastor and discussing the return of the Jews to Israel. At the time, I was wondering whether Israel's return to the Promised Land after nearly two thousand years was a testament to their arrogance and pig-headedness or whether it was truly the "Hand of God." I must be honest; at the time I was convinced of the former. Unbeknown to me, I was being sentimental to Replacement Theology.

During this conversation, the pastor simply asked me to explain Zechariah 12:10. "And I will pour on the House of David and on the inhabitants of Jerusalem the Spirit of grace and supplication; then they will look on Me whom they pierced."

This was the "a-ha" moment. It was at that moment that I realised Israel's return to the land had nothing to do with arrogance or pig-headedness and everything to do with the "Hand of God," His love for Israel, and a testament to the undeniable reality that God is not finished with her.

It was through this encounter that God began to open the fact that both anti-Semitism and replacement theology are tools the devil uses to thwart God and His plans and purposes.

## How Do We Explain Israel's Existence?

If God is finished with Israel, how can one explain the continuing existence of the Jewish people? Despite two millennia of persecution, the Jewish people remain. Despite the genocide of more than six million European Jews at the hands of the Nazis, the Jews remain to this day. How does one explain that, or Israel's rebirth, if one does not mention God?

## How Do We Explain the Rebirth of Israel?

After two thousand years of exile and persecution, in one day (May 14, 1948), Israel declared independence and a nation was reborn. This one act fulfilled a prophecy given more than 2,500 years ago:

> Who has heard such a thing?
> Who has seen such things?
> Shall the earth be made to give birth in one day?
> Or shall a nation be born at once?
> For as soon as Zion was in labour,
> She gave birth to her children. (Isaiah 66:8)

## How Do We Explain the Wars since Their Independence in 1948?

In chapter 8, we look at several wars designed to destroy the newly established nation. In each conflict, Israel ended up with more land. In 1948, the Jews were still struggling to stand after the holocaust of WWII, when they were invaded by vastly superior armies but won the war. Likewise, how do we explain Israel's victory in the 1967 Six-Day War and the liberation of Jerusalem, if not for God?

## How Can We Explain the Economic Growth and Military Might of Israel?

The *Jerusalem Post* article, dated May 10, 2016, states, "In 2015 Israel's GDP stood at NIS[3] 1,108.8 billion, 44 times greater than in 1950 (NIS 25.1 billion)." Economically, this is amazing. The opinion piece in the *Jerusalem Post* on May 11, 2016, highlights this:

> [W]e can look back at our achievements with pride, and look forward to our future with cautious optimism.
>
> The Israeli economy has grown 180 per cent over the past 20 years, while our population has increased by only 45 per cent.
> Our debt-to-GDP ratio is steadily falling, unemployment is lower than the OECD average and more and more Israelis are entering the workforce every day.
> Our optimism regarding the bright future of the Israeli economy is based on a number of Israel's relative advantages, namely:
>
> - Technology—Israel spends more money per capita on R&D than any other country in the world; 140 out of every 10,000 citizens work in R&D and cyber security.
> - Exports—In a study carried out by Global Entrepreneurship Monitor, Israel was ranked the top country for export-oriented entrepreneurial activity.
> - Demography—Israel has the youngest population of any OECD country (median age 31 and average age 42), the third most educated population that is growing faster than most other countries, and a positive migration rate.
> - High credit rating—Israel has an extremely high credit rating, in part because it was never in arrears on debt payments to suppliers or foreign lenders.[4]

These sentiments are further supported by Mark Twain. When speaking of the Jews he said,

> If the statistics are right, the Jews constitute but one-quarter of one percent of the human race. It suggests a nebulous puff of star dust lost in the blaze of the Milky Way. Properly, the Jew ought hardly to be heard of, but he is heard of, has always been heard of. He is as prominent on the planet as any other people, and his importance is extravagantly out of proportion to the smallness of his bulk.

His contributions to the world's list of great names in literature, science, art, music, finance, medicine and abstruse learning are also very out of proportion to the weakness of his numbers. He has made a marvellous fight in this world in all ages; and has done it with his hands tied behind him. He could be vain of himself and be excused for it. The Egyptians, the Babylonians and the Persians rose, filled the planet with sound and splendour, then faded to dream-stuff and passed away; the Greeks and Romans followed and made a vast noise, and they were gone; other people have sprung up and held their torch high for a time but it burned out, and they sit in twilight now, and have vanished.

The Jew saw them all, survived them all, and is now what he always was, exhibiting no decadence, no infirmities, of age, no weakening of his parts, no slowing of his energies, no dulling of his alert but aggressive mind. All things are mortal but the Jews; all other forces pass, but he remains. What is the secret of his immortality?[5]

## How Do We Explain All These Things?

It's called Covenant! God made an unconditional, everlasting covenant with Abraham.

It is called a Miracle! As Israel's first prime minister, David Ben Gurion, once said, "In Israel, in order to be a realist, you must believe in miracles"[6].

It is called a Blessing! God promised that He would bless Israel and the nations that bless her but would also curse nations that cursed her.

It is called a Promise! God promised that He would bring the nation home, including the so-called lost tribes of Israel. And He is faithful to His promises.

God has a covenant with Israel, and He has promised to bless her. So despite all the hatred, and being only 22,000 km² with a population of just 6 million people, Israel has been blessed. She has the thirty-sixth largest economy in the world.

Since that "a-ha" moment, in 2014 I had the privilege of going to Israel and travelling around Galilee, Megiddo, Masada, and Kumran. It proved an amazing experience. However, the high-point was going to the Western Wall and seeing thousands of devout Jews praying at their holiest site, in their capital, Jerusalem. A Jew there told me that they are all praying for the promised Messiah to come. As a believer in Jesus, I am longing for His return, so in a very real sense, we are seeking the same thing!

When Jesus was on the earth, He linked Israel's exile directly to the national rejection of Him as their Messiah.

> For days will come upon you when your enemies will build an embankment around you, surround you and close you in on every side, and level you, and your children within you, to the ground; and they will not leave in you one stone upon another, because you did not know the time of your visitation. (Luke 19:43–44)

Israel has not yet, as a nation, accepted Yeshua[7] as their long-awaited Messiah. So why then, I questioned, would God bring them home? That was my problem. However, the pastor showed me that when Israel is dwelling in the land, only then will they recognise the Messiah when God pours out the Spirit of Grace and Supplication on them.[8]

One last thought. In Psalm 119:111 (NASB), we read, "I have inherited Your testimonies forever, for they are the joy of my heart."

The testimony of the goodness, the grace, the favour, the love, the power, and the promises of God for His covenant people becomes my story too. If God has done marvellous things for Israel and His chosen people, He will do the same for a "Gentile" like me. I have been grafted into the vine, and I have become a partaker of the root and fatness of the olive tree.[9] When we read of His protection of Israel over millennia, we know He will protect us too. When we read of the restoration of Israel and its rebirth in a day, we know He can bring breakthrough and deliverance to us too.

This ultimately is a book that will build the faith of all believers in Jesus (Yeshua), and I pray it will challenge the thinking of unbelievers.

# ACKNOWLEDGMENTS

I would like to thank all those whose assistance and encouragement proved to be invaluable in the accomplishment of this book. Without their input, support and encouragement this book would never have been written.

My wife, Olga, who encouraged me to write because she believed I had something significant to say and helped me overcome the feelings of inadequacy when it came to writing this book.

Daryl, whose love for Israel was an inspiration and who was the reason for travelling to Israel the first time that truly impacted my life.

My daughter, Kristy and son-in-law, Caleb, who encouraged me to keep going when I felt it was all too much.

Suzanne who dedicated a lot of time to help edit the manuscript and make it readable for the publishers.

Pastor George Halik, my brother-in-law and sister-in-law, Sophie, who are both mentors and inspirations to me. It was George who asked the question that changed my understanding of Israel.

My church family at Gippsland Christian Church for their love and support.

# SECTION 1

# GOD'S COVENANT PEOPLE

# CHAPTER 1
## Hosea: Why Care about Israel?

*[My] chiropodist was a Jew who has so many times "put me upon my feet," that I would have no objection to giving his countrymen "a leg up."*

—Abraham Lincoln (US president, 1861–1865)

Israel is a land of just 22,000 square kilometres with a population of 8 million people (6 million Jews) in the midst of a region that measures 8,804,395 square kilometres and a population of almost 412 million. Just 2 per cent of the region's population live in 2 per cent of the region, yet Israel remains a hotbed of trouble and vitriol. So why care about Israel? And why stand united with it?

We care because God cares.

Throughout the Bible, we read of God's unconditional love for Israel. He describes it as His special treasure, His bride, and the apple of His eye, despite the nation's constant sin and rebellion.

The prophet Hosea says,

> When Israel was a child, I [God] loved him, and out of Egypt I called My son ... I drew them with gentle cords, with bands of love, and I was to them as those who take the yoke from their neck. I stooped and fed them ... How can I give you up, Ephraim? How can I hand you over, Israel? ... My heart churns within Me; My sympathy is stirred. (Hosea 11:1, 4, 8)

Why care about Israel? Why love Israel? The answer is simple: because God has always cared for and loved Israel.

Jesus showed His love for the nation, the very nation that rejected Him, when days before the cross He lamented over Jerusalem as He looked down from the Temple Mount.

> O Jerusalem, Jerusalem, the one who kills the prophets and stones those who are sent to her! How often I wanted to gather your children together, as a hen gathers her chicks under her wings, but you were not willing! See! Your house is left to you desolate; for I say to you, you shall see Me no more till you say, "Blessed is He who comes in the name of the Lord!" (Matthew 23:37–39)

Ezekiel 16 is a graphic picture of God's love for Jerusalem and how He caused it to thrive and flourish; yet, it rebelled. Despite all its shortcomings, sins, and acts of rebellion, God has always remained faithful and promises to remember His covenant. He never abandoned or ceased to love it, and we too have an obligation not to abandon or stop loving Israel.

## Renounce past injustices, and live out of love and solidarity.

We stand united with Israel because God loves her. We recognise that everything God loves, the devil hates. Standing with Israel means we stand against the attacks of its enemies.

In the past, the church has had a poor record of standing with Israel against the attacks of the enemy. The sad reality is that the church has aided and abetted anti-Semitic attitudes and behaviours all the way back to the second century.

The church has been charged with the task of "provoking the Jews to jealousy" (Romans 11:11) but has driven a wedge between itself and the Jews and between the Jews and their Messiah.

Paul says that the Jews cannot see their Messiah because a veil is over their eyes.[10] It is the church's task to aid them to remove it; however, rather than helping to remove the veil, the church's actions have added further layers to the spiritual veil and made their blindness worse.

There are so many examples of the church's hatred towards the Jews. The Eastern Church, the Roman Catholic Church, and the Protestant churches have all practised anti-Semitism. Here are a few examples of the early church's hatred of the Jew:

> For if we are still practicing Judaism, we admit that we have not received God's favour ... It is wrong to talk about Jesus Christ and live like Jews. For Christianity did not believe in Judaism, but Judaism in Christianity. (Ignatius, bishop of Antioch, AD 98–117)[11]

> Take heed to yourselves and be not like some piling up your sins and saying that the covenant is theirs as well as ours. It is ours, but they lost it completely just after Moses received it. ("Epistle of Barnabas," 4:6–7, between AD 130 and 138)[12]

> The synagogue is worse than a brothel ... It is the den of scoundrels and the repair of wild beasts ... the temple of demons devoted to idolatrous cults ... the refuge of brigands and dabauchees, and the cavern of devils. It is a criminal assembly of Jews ... a place of meeting for the assassins of Christ ... a house worse than a drinking shop ... a den of thieves, a house of ill fame, a dwelling of iniquity, the refuge of devils, a gulf and an abyss of perdition ... I would say the same things about their souls ... As for me, I hate the synagogue ... I hate the Jews for

the same reason. (John Chrysostom, AD 344–407)[13]

Just as in the Eastern Church, history shows that the Roman Catholic Church is also guilty of anti-Semitic behaviour. For example, in 538, the Third Synod of Orléans made a decree that Jews could not show themselves in the streets during Passover Week. How disgusting. During one of the holiest feasts on the Jewish calendar, the church made Jews virtual prisoners in their own homes. Some one hundred and fifty years later, at the Synod of Toledo, cardinals ordered the burning of the Talmud and other Jewish books. And in 937, at the behest of Pope Leo VII, the archbishop of Mainz expelled all Jews who refused to be baptised. Pope Paul IV, in 1555, banished the Jews to ghettos and decreed that they were to wear distinctive head coverings to separate them from the rest of society.

The Protestant churches are not exempt either. Martin Luther asked, "What shall we Christians do with this rejected and condemned people, the Jews?"

He then proceeded to answer his own question.

1. Set fire to their synagogues and schools.
2. Destroy Jewish houses.
3. Destroy all their prayer books and Talmudic writings.
4. Forbid rabbis from teaching, on pain of loss of life and limb.
5. Abolish safe conduct on highways completely for the Jews.
6. Confiscate all cash, silver, and gold from Jews.
7. Expel Jews from the country.[14]

There were times when the church allowed Jews to exercise freedom of religion and assembly, but all too often persecution was at the fore. The Christian community needs to acknowledge these past injustices, apologise, and live out of love for the people that God chose and loves.

There is, of course, this argument: "These were the actions of past generations, or even different denominations, and I am not responsible for them." That is true, but the acknowledgement of wrong brings healing and a commitment not to replicate the sins of the past. Daniel is a great example of this. He recognised that the Jewish exile in Babylon was almost over, so he prayed and fasted in sackcloth and ashes, and he made the following confession:

> O Lord, great and awesome God, who keeps His covenant and mercy with those who love Him, and with those who keep His commandments, we have sinned and committed iniquity, we have done wickedly and rebelled, even by departing from Your precepts and Your judgments. Neither

> have we heeded Your servants the prophets, who spoke in Your name to our kings and our princes, to our fathers and all the people of the land. (Daniel 9:3–6)

From what we are told of Daniel, he never rebelled, never committed wicked acts, never departed from God's law, and never ignored the prophets, yet his prayer was that *we* have sinned and committed these acts. Despite his innocence in the Jews' sin, he associated with them. The church needs to associate with the wicked deeds done to Israel in the name of the church, repent, and stand united with Israel.

## Spiritual Debt to Jews

The third reason to care for Israel is that the church is indebted to her.

> For it pleased those from Macedonia and Achaia to make a certain contribution for the poor among the saints who are in Jerusalem. It pleased them indeed, and they are their debtors. For if the Gentiles have been partakers of their spiritual things, their duty is also to minister to them in material things. (Romans 15:26–27)

It was the father of the nation, Abraham, whose obedience to God led to a covenant of blessing from which Gentiles now benefit.

> Christ has redeemed us from the curse of the law, having become a curse for us (for it is written, "Cursed is everyone who hangs on a tree"), that the blessing of Abraham might come upon the Gentiles in Christ Jesus, that we might receive the promise of the Spirit through faith. (Galatians 3:13–14)

We cannot deny or escape the Jewish roots of our faith. Nor can we ignore the great debt we owe to the Jews. Scripture states, "Salvation is from the Jews."[15] These are Jesus' words, not mine. Jesus is not negating the fact that He is the only way to be saved, but in God's plan of salvation, He chose Israel as His instrument to bring the Saviour into the world.

Scripture also states that our Saviour's identity is forever Jewish. For eternity, Jesus is to be called "the Son of David." Scripture further states that all of the apostles were Jews and all of the scriptures were written by Jews. The only possible exception is Luke, who might have been a Greek. But Greek or not, it is of little consequence, because Luke was a companion of Paul, a Jew, and was well versed in the Old Testament scriptures.

This doesn't excuse their mistakes, but as friends and family, we support them. In Romans 10:19 and 11:30–31, Paul sums up our spiritual debt to Israel by reminding us that Gentile believers were once disobedient to God yet have now obtained mercy and become obedient to the truth because of Israel's disobedience.

One of the ways we can begin to "repay" our debt is to assist the Jews in fulfilling the great end-time prophecy that they will once again be in their own land. Scripture makes it clear that the Gentiles are invited to participate with God in this process.

> Thus says the Lord God:
> "Behold, I will lift My hand in an oath to the nations,
> And set up My standard for the peoples;
> They shall bring your sons in their arms,
> And your daughters shall be carried on their shoulders" (Isaiah 49:22)

The International Christian Embassy in Jerusalem, which works to assist Jews in relocating back in their homeland, has in its mandate this very passage.

A day is coming when that debt will be "paid in full," when our righteousness, obtained through faith, will provoke the Jew to pursue righteousness by faith and not by works.

> What then shall we say? That the Gentiles, who did not pursue righteousness, have obtained it, a righteousness that is by faith; but the people of Israel, who pursued the law as the way of righteousness, have not attained their goal. (Romans 9:30–31)

Then together we will see the great end-time revival sweep the land of Israel.[16] This will be such a powerful move of God that all other revivals will pale in comparison. As glorious as those revivals were, Paul says this move of God will be "life from the dead."[17]

## Spiritual enrichment

Our spiritual enrichment, like our salvation, is because of the Jews. We are branches that have grafted into Israel, we have never replaced her. Paul explains this in Romans 11 when he says,

> But some of these branches from Abraham's tree—some of the people of Israel —have been broken off. And you Gentiles, who were branches from a wild olive tree, have been grafted in. So now you also receive the blessing God has promised Abraham and his children, sharing in the rich nourishment from the root of God's special olive tree. (Romans 11:17, NLT)

One of the significant statements, tying Israel to the church, is Paul's declaration that the wild olive (the Gentiles) has been grafted in to the natural olive (the Jews). The church is a graft into the nation of Israel. Paul adds in verse 18, "[D]o not boast against the branches. But if you do boast, remember that you do not support the root, but the root supports you."

Paul tells us that there is nothing to boast about in being grafted into Israel. We are not better than Israel; in fact, the church's life is inextricably linked to hers. Like any natural graft, the rootstock supports the graft, not the other way around. The nourishment needed by all plants come from the rootstock. The roots draw the food to the branches, and the sun converts the food to life. Just as in a natural tree, a healthy root system is needed to supply the leaves with the necessary ingredients for the sun and air to cause growth, the church needs the root system provided by the Jews in combination with the Son and the Spirit to bring life.

Here, Paul is suggesting that the health of the church depends on the care she shows for Israel. I know God is not finished with Israel, for which I am grateful, because if He has, there is no hope for the church. We will examine this idea in chapter 3, because if Israel "is dead" to God, then so too is the church.

## Genesis 12:3 Still Applies

> I will bless those who bless you,
> And I will curse him who curses you;
> And in you all the families of the earth shall be blessed. (Genesis 12:3)

In the next chapter, we will look at the covenant that God made with Abraham; for now, let it suffice to say that the promise with Abraham has never been made void. God still blesses those people and nations that bless, love, and care for Israel. And the opposite is still true: He curses the people and nations that curse, hate, and do not care for Israel.

> "For behold, in those days and at that time,
> When I bring back the captives of Judah and Jerusalem,
> I will also gather all nations,
> And bring them down to the Valley of Jehoshaphat;
> And I will enter into judgment with them there
> On account of My people, My heritage Israel,
> Whom they have scattered among the nations;
> They have also divided up My land.
> They have cast lots for My people,
> Have given a boy as payment for a harlot,
> And sold a girl for wine, that they may drink.

> "Indeed, what have you to do with Me,
> O Tyre and Sidon, and all the coasts of Philistia?
> Will you retaliate against Me?
> But if you retaliate against Me,
> Swiftly and speedily I will return your retaliation upon your own head;
> Because you have taken My silver and My gold,
> And have carried into your temples My prized possessions.
> Also the people of Judah and the people of Jerusalem
> You have sold to the Greeks,
> That you may remove them far from their borders.
> "Behold, I will raise them
> Out of the place to which you have sold them,
> And will return your retaliation upon your own head.
> I will sell your sons and your daughters
> Into the hand of the people of Judah,
> And they will sell them to the Sabeans,
> To a people far off;
> For the Lord has spoken." (Joel 3:1–8)

In these eight verses, we see that God associates Himself with both the people and the land of Israel, calling the land "My land" and the Israelites "My people." He is bringing them home and will judge the nations that have exiled His people and divided their land. He then signals out Lebanon (Tyre, Sidon) and Gaza (Philista) for special mention and promises to judge them for their part in persecuting Israel.

Jesus confirmed this when he said all the nations are going to appear before Him to give an account of their treatment of "His brethren." He is not referring to the church. The church did not exist at this point. He is speaking about a judgement on the nations as to how they treated His "natural" brethren, the nation of Israel.

## Jesus' Return Is Tied to Israel

Like all Christians, we are longing for Jesus' return. Romans 8:19 says that all of creation is looking with eagerness for His return. Meanwhile, in Corinthians, Paul tells us the church is eager for His return.

> Therefore, you do not lack any spiritual gift as you eagerly wait for our Lord Jesus Christ to be revealed. (1 Corinthians 1:7)

Jesus says He is coming soon and the New Testament closes out with this cry, "Amen, come, Lord Jesus."

For all our longing and watching with eager anticipation for His return, Jesus tells us exactly when He will return.

> For I say to you, you shall see Me no more till you say, "Blessed is He who comes in the name of the Lord!" (Matthew 23:39)

It is only when Israel's spiritual leaders are living in Jerusalem and cry out in faith to Yeshua (Jesus), *"Baruch ha-ba b'shem Adonai,"* will Jesus return, having been invited back by the Jews.[18]

## Conclusion

We should care about Israel because God cares for her. The church benefits from loving Israel. Our roots are deep in Judaism, our spiritual fruitfulness is tied to our treatment of Israel, and our desire for Jesus to return quickly is tied to a spiritual awakening and heartfelt cry of the Jews for Jesus to return to Jerusalem.

Christians are indebted to the Jewish people. The Jews have given us everything we believe in, the Bible, the Apostles and even Jesus Himself is Jewish. Yet throughout history, the church has frequently rejected and persecuted the Jews. We should be deeply ashamed of that aspect of our past.

Today we have a unique opportunity to reverse the wrongs of the last two thousand years and write a new chapter in the relationship between the church and the Jewish people. Now is the time to bless them. Now is the time to assist them return to the land God promised them as an everlasting and unconditional possession.

# CHAPTER 2
## Genesis—It All Started with Abraham

*The Bible is our mandate!*

—David Ben-Gurion (before the Peel Commission)

While the return of Jews to Israel started en masse in the early 1800s and continues to this day, the real story began almost four thousand years ago, when God appeared to Abraham's father, Terah, and told him to leave his home in Ur of the Chaldeans, a city in modern-day Iraq, and go to Canaan.

> And Terah took his son Abram and his grandson Lot, the son of Haran, and his daughter-in-law Sarai, his son Abram's wife, and they went out with them from Ur of the Chaldeans to go to the land of Canaan; and they came to Haran and dwelt there. So the days of Terah were two hundred and five years, and Terah died in Haran. (Genesis 11:31–32)

Terah only got as far as Haran, in southern Turkey, where he lived until he died. After his death, the Lord told Abraham to complete the journey to the Promised Land.

> "Get out of your country,
> From your family
> And from your father's house,
> To a land that I will show you.
> I will make you a great nation.
> I will bless you
> And make your name great;
> And you shall be a blessing.
> I will bless those who bless you,
> And I will curse him who curses you;
> And in you all the families of the earth shall be blessed." (Genesis 12:1–3)

God promised Abraham that if he left Haran, He would do four things for him and his descendants.

### Firstly, God Promised to Give Abraham a Land

God promised that if he left Haran and his family, he would be shown a new land that would be his descendant's special possession. Some two thousand years later, writing to Hebrew believers in Jesus, the Apostle Paul wrote,

> By faith Abraham obeyed when he was called to go out to the place which he would receive as an inheritance. And he went out, not knowing where he was going. By faith he dwelt in the land of promise as in a foreign country, dwelling in tents with Isaac and Jacob, the heirs with him of the same promise. (Hebrews 11:8–9)

Abraham is promised a land but was not told its borders. He would however recognise it when he arrived. On arriving in the land, God reiterated the promise in Genesis 15 but this time He clearly defined the borders.

> "To your descendants I have given this land, from the river of Egypt to the great river, the River Euphrates …" (Genesis 15:18)

God set the borders from the Nile River in the south to the Euphrates in the north and from the Mediterranean Sea in the west to the Jordan River in the east.

The Hebrews then spent over four hundred years as slaves in Egypt while the land promised to Abraham was occupied by several hostile nations. After leaving Egypt, and on the verge of ending forty years of wandering in the wilderness that surrounded the Promised Land, God reaffirmed the boundaries to Joshua:

> "From the wilderness and this Lebanon as far as the great river, the River Euphrates, all the land of the Hittites, and to the Great Sea toward the going down of the sun, shall be your territory." (Joshua 1:4)

Under the reigns of King David and King Solomon, Israel came close to dwelling in the land that God promised, but because of sin and rebellion, God at times exiled them or allowed their enemies to invade. In all that time, He always remained faithful to His covenant with Abraham, by raising up leaders to defeat the invaders or by bringing them home, or promising one day to bring them home.

## Secondly, God Promises Abraham a Nation

The promise of land was observable, not so the nation. Abraham was seventy-five years old when God told him to go to the land that he would inherit. In that land, God was going to use Abraham and Sarah to birth a nation that would become God's treasured possession[19] and the "apple of His eye."[20]

This was problematic because God made this promise to Abraham when he was seventy-five years old. Ten years later, he still had no heir. Abraham was fully aware of the problem and told God that because he didn't have a son, his Syrian servant would inherit all his possessions. God responded by telling Abraham that his servant, Eliezer, would not inherit the promise and that he would indeed have a son.[21]

## The Abrahamic Covenant

To confirm His commitment to the promise, God didn't just say it; He bound Himself to the promise by making a blood covenant.

> "Bring Me a three-year-old heifer, a three-year-old female goat, a three-year-old ram, a turtledove, and a young pigeon." Then he brought all these to Him and cut them in two, down the middle, and placed each piece opposite the other; but he did not cut the birds in two. (Genesis 15:9, 10)

The scene would look grotesque to modern-day observers—five bloody animal carcasses on the ground, three of them split in half, with the halves separated a short distance from each other. In Abraham's time, the arrangement of divided animal carcasses would have been instantly recognised as the preparation for a blood covenant, where two kings "cut" a covenant that bound them together by promises made and oaths taken.

While the preparations would have been recognisable, what followed differed markedly from the usual.

## Covenants Always Began with a Statement of the Terms Agreed Upon

Both parties to a covenant agree on the terms of the agreement; however, in this case, while God spoke and made promises, Abraham remained silent. With Abraham silent, God agreed to two things.

Firstly, Abraham would indeed have a son (Genesis 15:4), and the descendants of his son would inherit all the land within the boundaries outlined in Genesis 15:7, 18.

Yet because of Abraham's silence, he didn't bind himself or his descendants after him to keep any agreement. The terms of this covenant are all one way. God is unconditionally favouring Abraham and his descendants.

## Covenants Are Ratified by some Solemn, Ritual and External

## Actions

Once the terms are agreed upon, the covenant is ratified when both parties walk between the slaughtered animals, binding each other to the terms of the covenant.

While Abraham was waiting for God, so together they could both pass between the sacrifice, something else that is unusual with covenants happened:

> Now when the sun was going down, a deep sleep fell upon Abram; and behold, horror and great darkness fell upon him ... And it came to pass, when the sun went down and it was dark, that behold, there appeared a smoking oven and a burning torch that passed between those pieces. (Genesis 15:12, 17)

God caused a deep sleep to come on Abraham, and while he slept God passed between the sacrifice, alone, binding Himself to the promises of the covenant while Abraham was under no obligation to them.

God set terms to the agreement and bound himself to keep them. The terms of that covenant are outlined in Genesis 15:18–21.

> On the same day the Lord made a covenant with Abram, saying, "To your descendants I have given this land, from the river of Egypt to the great river, the River Euphrates—the Kenites, the Kenezzites, the Ammonites, the Hittites, the Perizzites, the Rephaim, the Amorites, the Canaanites, the Girgashites, and the Jebusites."

This covenant can only be voided if God is unfaithful. It can never be voided by Israel's unbelief. God remains faithful to the covenant because He cannot deny Himself. Paul says,

> "If we are faithless, He remains faithful; He cannot deny Himself." (2 Timothy 2:13)

## Each Party Takes an Oath to Observe the Terms

After agreeing to and ratifying the terms of the covenant, both parties swear to keep the promises they have made. Abraham was not obligated to make such an oath, because he never made a promise nor did he pass between the carcasses.

God shows the depth of His commitment to this covenant when he says in Jeremiah 31, only if the moon, the sun and the stars stop shining will the agreement He's made with Abraham cease to exist (see Jeremiah 31:35, 36).

The Apostle Paul says that, "God swore by himself" and Abraham patiently endured until he received the promise.

> For when God made a promise to Abraham, because He could swear by no one greater, He swore by Himself, saying, "Surely blessing I will bless you, and multiplying I will multiply you." And so, after he had patiently endured, he obtained the promise. (Hebrews 6:13–15)

The covenant God made with Abraham was unlike any other. This agreement was not conditional upon Israel's faithfulness; it was solely dependent upon God faithfully keeping His agreed terms.

## A Curse Is on Any Party That Breaks the Agreement

What if the oath is broken and the promises are not kept? During Biblical times, a curse is pronounced on the party to the covenant who breaks their word by declaring to each other, "If I break any terms in this covenant, may the same thing happen to me as happened to the animals."[22]

As we have seen, Abraham made no commitment. Nor did he ratify the agreement; therefore, he cannot be cursed.

On the other hand, if God casts off Israel and the sun still shines, then God has broken His oath; and because of the strength of covenant, this would bring a curse upon Himself. How absurd, even for a microsecond, to contemplate that thought!

All through Scripture a thread runs, and that thread is the faithfulness of God to His promises. Paul asks the questions:

> What if some were unfaithful? Does their faithlessness nullify the faithfulness of God? (Romans 3:3)

The answer is obvious. Israel's unfaithfulness does not nullify God's faithfulness. In Psalms and Deuteronomy, we find the following:

> He has remembered His mercy and His faithfulness to the house of Israel. (Psalm 98:3)

> Therefore know that the LORD your God, He is God, the faithful God, who keeps His covenant and His mercy for a thousand generations with those who love Him and keep His commandments. (Deuteronomy 7:9)

Considering a generation is forty years, this indicates a time span of 40,000 years. This is not speaking of the Abrahamic covenant but the covenant with Moses, and it shows that God is faithful to keep His covenants.

## Mosaic Covenant

Around five hundred years after the Abrahamic Covenant, following four hundred years of exile, Israel left Egypt and was camped at the foot of Mount Sinai. From there, God called Moses up the mountain and told him to tell the people to keep the covenant.

The only covenant they had was the Abrahamic covenant. That covenant bought them freedom. It was a covenant of faith. It was the covenant of grace. God was telling Israel to live by faith in His promises.

However, in Exodus 19:8, when the Hebrews said, "All that the Lord has spoken we will do," everything changed. The Israelites would no longer live by faith but by works of obedience. In response to that oath the law was given.

As we have seen, in covenant, there is both blessing and curse: a blessing for keeping covenant and a curse for breaking it. In Deuteronomy 28, there is the blessing and curse. If Israel lived up to their oath—a blessing (Deuteronomy 28:1-14); however, if they failed to live up to the oath—a curse (Deuteronomy 28:15-68), and a part of the curse is being driven from the land that was promised to them through the Abrahamic covenant.

> "You shall beget sons and daughters, but they shall not be yours; for they shall go into captivity ... And the Lord will take you back to Egypt in ships, by the way of which I said to you, 'You shall never see it again.' And there you shall be offered for sale to your enemies as male and female slaves, but no one will buy you." (Deuteronomy 28:41, 68)

When Israel was exiled, it was because they couldn't live up to its oath to "do whatever He says." A curse was brought on the nation because of their failure to live by the Mosaic Covenant.

When God bought them back, it was always because of His faithfulness to the Abrahamic Covenant. Zechariah 9:11-12 makes that point very clearly:

> "As for you also,
> Because of the blood of your covenant,
> I will set your prisoners free from the waterless pit.
> Return to the stronghold,
> You prisoners of hope.
> Even today I declare
> That I will restore double to you."

## Abraham's Two Sons

After God established the covenant with Abraham, another year goes by and he still has no heir. Sarah was unable to have children and so she devised a plan to "help God" make it happen. She had Abraham father a child with her servant Hagar with the intention of raising him as her own (see Genesis 16:1, 2). Ishmael was born and from him a nation, but not the nation of promise. That would take another thirteen years.

As for Ishmael, God blessed him because of his father Abraham but says,

> He shall be a wild man, his hand shall be against every man, and every man's hand against him. (Genesis 16:12)

> And he shall dwell in the presence of all his brethren. And as for Ishmael, I have heard you. Behold, I have blessed him, and will make him fruitful, and will multiply him exceedingly. He shall beget twelve princes, and I will make him a great nation. (Genesis 17:20)

The twelve princes of Ishmael are the ancestors of the Arab people, and while we certainly do see conflict between the Arabs and Jews, there seems to be a never-ending conflict amongst themselves.

## Islam's Prophet Abraham

In Islam, Prophet Ibrahim (Abraham) is the friend of God and the father of all the Prophets, which makes Muhammad a direct descendant of Abraham.

Anyone who rejects the Prophet Abraham is not a true believer in Islam.

Adherents to Islam hold to the "five pillars of Islam" that form their fundamental doctrines. They also form the basis of the Muslim life. These pillars are as follows:

1. Faith (the profession that there is only one God, Allah, and that Muhammad is God's messenger)
2. Prayer (the obligatory five daily prayers)
3. Charity (the practice of charitable giving based on accumulated wealth)
4. Fasting (an obligation during the month of Ramadan)
5. Hajj (the pilgrimage to Mecca)

Two of the five pillars show the high esteem that Islam has for Abraham. They also show that Islam is a perversion of Judaism and Muslims have an ongoing historic connection to land.

The second pillar is prayer. Every Muslim from teenage years onward is obliged to pray five times a day. In each of these five prayers, Muslims at some point must ask Allah to send His blessings upon the Prophet Ibrahim. Millions of people, five times a day, ask *Allah* to bless Abraham. This shows the high regard Islam has for Abraham. The fifth and most well known pillar of Islam is the pilgrimage to Mecca, called the Hajj, which occurs during the Islamic month of Dhu al-Hijjah.

Every able-bodied Muslim is obliged to make the pilgrimage to Mecca at least once in his or her lifetime.

The Prophet Ibrahim is central to this fifth pillar, for even Muhammad said so: "You must adhere to the traditions and rituals (of Hajj), for these have come down to you from your forefather *Ibrahim*."

Firstly, no Hajj is valid without going around the Kaaba in a counter-clockwise direction seven times. The Kaaba is a building at the centre of Islam's most sacred mosque, Al-Masjid Al-Harāmis, in Mecca. Muslims believe it was built by Prophets Ibrahim (Abraham) and Ismail (Ishmael).

Secondly, during the Hajj, Muslims run between Safa and Marwa (two hills close to the Kaaba) seven times to commemorate their belief that it was here that Ibrahim left Hagar and Ishmael to test their faith.

According to the Koran, the Prophet Abraham lived with his wife and son in the valley of Mecca by God's order to pioneer a civilization. It was within this civilization that the Prophet Mohammed was born.

> And when we made the House (at Mecca) a resort for mankind and sanctuary, (saying): Take as your place of worship the place where Abraham stood (to pray). And We imposed a duty upon Abraham and Ishmael, (saying): Purify My house for those who go around and those who meditate therein and those who bow down and prostrate themselves (in worship). (Sura 2:125)

> And when Abraham and Ishmael were raising the foundations of the House, (Abraham prayed): Our Lord! Accept from us (this duty). Lo! Thou, only Thou, art the Hearer, the Knower. (Sura 2:127)

What is the Arab connection to Abraham? According to their sacred text, Abraham, along with his wife Hagar and son Ishmael, headed into Arabia and came to Mecca. There they built a home, and it is there that Abraham was willing to sacrifice Ishmael.

While Jews and Christians believe that the Bible is the true word of God and reject out of hand this tradition, Muslims cannot. Their five pillars and the sacrifice at Eid-ul-Adha are all centred on this tradition. They believe that Abraham lived in Arabia and use this to explain the birth of Muhammad, a direct descendant of Abraham, who was born in Mecca.

Muslims own sacred texts show that Arabs have an historic and ongoing connection to the land of Arabia and not to Israel.

Jews and Christians say that God has blessed Ishmael, but the covenant is with Isaac.

## Israel's Father, Abraham

When Abraham went to God and said "I have no heir," and that his servant, Eliezer of Damascus, was the rightful heir of Abraham's fortune, God said that his own son would inherit, and that son was Isaac, whose mother was Sarah.

> "My covenant I will establish with Isaac, whom Sarah shall bear to you at this set time next year." (Genesis 17:21)

Both Judaism and Islam claim Abraham as "their own," and both religions have strong connections to land.

However, Israel's claim is in Israel and Jerusalem, while the Arab's claim is in Arabia and Mecca. The Arab nations have no ongoing connection to Israel, just as Jews have no ongoing connection to Arabia.

## Thirdly, God Promises to Bless Abraham

The word "blessed" carries a host of meanings, including happy, fortunate, and favoured. God is saying that Abraham's seed is to be highly favoured and prosperous. When we consider the impact that this tiny nation has had on the world, we see that the blessing of God is certainly on Israel.

What God blesses the devil seeks to curse.

## Fourthly, the Nations of the World's Fortunes Are Linked to Abraham

The nations of the world will either be blessed or cursed depending on how they treat Israel. If the nations bless Israel, they will be blessed; if they curse Israel, they will be cursed.[23]

Jesus pointed this out in the parable of the sheep and the goats, recorded in Matthew 25. The nations will be assembled before the throne of judgement, and Jesus will sort them, sheep on one side and the goats on the other. To the sheep He will say, "Come Blessed of my Father, enter into your kingdom." But to the goats He will say, "Depart from Me, you cursed, into the everlasting fire prepared for the devil and his angels."

The blessed nations will ask, "Why are we blessed?" while the cursed nations will ask Him, "Why are we cursed?" The answer is the same; they are being judged according to how they treated Jesus' brethren, the Jews.

## UNESCO's Appalling Resolution

On October 25, 2016, the United Nations Educational, Scientific, and Cultural Organization (UNESCO) passed an appalling resolution that denies both Jewish and Christian cultural links to Jerusalem and the Temple Mount. The resolution was put forward by a group of Arab nations, at the behest of the Palestinian Authority. It refers to the Old City of Jerusalem and the Temple Mount only by its Islamic name, Al-Haram Al-Sharif, and was passed by a count of ten for, two against, eight abstentions, and one nation not present. In response, Israel's ambassador to UNESCO, Carmel Shama-Hacohen, said, "This is the garbage, this is the resolution, and this is the place for it" as he pointed to the trash can. As he dropped it in the trash he added,

> On one hand it will become one with similar resolutions adopted with regards to the Jewish people. On the other hand, it might get a bit crowded between uncountable UN Human Rights Council resolutions, the UN in New York and other diabolical ideologies for the destruction of Israel devised by past empires and dictators not worthy of us mentioning them. All of which have this in common—they all disappeared of the stage of history, existing no more, while the people of Israel are alive and well and a blue and white flag with the Star of David—Magen David—waving above our Jerusalem, our eternal and united capital.[24]

## Conclusion

Abraham is a prominent figure in all three religions central to the conflict in Israel. To the Muslims, he is a great prophet who went to live in Mecca in the region of Arabia, and to Christians and Jews, he is the father of the nation, Israel.

Abraham and Isaac settled in Canaan (Israel), while Ishmael and Abraham (according to Muslims) settled in Arabia. And so, in terms of the land of Israel, only one nation has an ongoing connection to the land, the Hebrews.

David Ben Gurion put it, when speaking before the Peel Commission in 1937, having been challenged about the Jews ongoing connection to the land, simply pointed to the Bible and said, "This is our mandate."

God made an eternal, unconditional covenant with Abraham that He would be a father of a nation and that He was giving Abraham's descendants, Isaac and Jacob (Israel) the land, known as the "Land of Promise."

Another covenant, the Law, came some six hundred years later but never voided the original, because the second, unlike the first, was neither eternal nor unconditional. This covenant given to Moses had a specific life. Jeremiah says a new covenant is coming that will supersede the Sinai covenant.[25]

There were times when Israel was exiled because of the curse associated with the Mosaic Covenant, but God always bought them home, or has promised to bring them back, because of the Abrahamic Covenant, the last time in 1948.

# CHAPTER 3

## The Heresy of Replacement Theology

*Israel's promises remain Israel's promises!*

—Jürgen Moltmann

Replacement Theology proposes that the church has replaced Israel as God's "treasured possession." At its core is the belief that because the Jews rejected Jesus as their Messiah, God has rejected them and made the church His chosen people. All Israel's promises and blessings of the Old Testament are now being fulfilled in the Christian Church.

Here listed are the four basic tenets of this heresy.

1. The Jewish people are no longer God's chosen people.
2. After Pentecost, the term "Israel" refers to the church.
3. The Mosaic covenant (Exodus 20) is replaced by the new covenant (Luke 22:20).
4. Actual circumcision is replaced by a circumcision of the heart (Romans 2:29).

The church has been involved in many atrocities and pogroms over the past two thousand years. [26] The pogroms of Russia at the end of the nineteenth century were carried out by Orthodox Christians, which convinced the Zionist Movement that the Jews needed to return to their own state in Palestine.

In Nazi Germany, schoolchildren were sent to see the Judensau on German churches.[27]

The only way to justify these, and countless other, examples of anti-Semitism in the church is to believe that the Jews are no longer God's treasured possession and that they are now cursed because the church has replaced Israel as God's chosen people.

The church does have a fuller revelation of God's redemptive plan, recognising that the long-awaited Jewish Messiah, Jesus (or Yeshua) has already come and that salvation is found in no other name.

However, that does not mean that God is finished with the Jews. As we saw in the previous chapter, God made a covenant with Abraham that is eternal and is unconditional. Because of that, the Jews remain God's treasured people, while the church has been grafted in. Below are ten reasons why Replacement Theology is wrong and needs to be rejected.

## The Old Testament Explicitly Teaches the Restoration of the Nation Israel.

There are so many promises in both the New and the Old Testaments of a future restoration of the Jewish people, which only makes sense if we believe that God has not rejected the Jews.

> And it shall come to pass in that day
> That the Lord shall set his hand again the second time
> To recover the remnant of his people, which shall be left,
> From Assyria, and Egypt,
> From Pathros, and Cush,
> From Elam, and Shinar,
> From Hamath, and the islands of the sea. (Isaiah 11:11)

> Fear not, for I am with you;
> I will bring your descendants from the east,
> And gather you from the west;
> I will say to the north, 'Give them up!'
> And to the south, 'Do not keep them back!'
> Bring My sons from afar,
> And My daughters from the ends of the earth.
> (Isaiah 43:5, 6)

Isaiah prophesied a much larger return than occurred when Judah returned from Babylon. These prophesies specifically mention Assyria who took the ten northern tribes captive. Those tribes are colloquially termed the "lost tribes" because they never returned from exile and seem lost to history. Isaiah says a day is coming when they will return. Likewise, Egypt, Sudan,[28] and others are mentioned as areas from which no Jews have returned, yet.

Not only Isaiah but Jeremiah, Ezekiel, Zechariah, Amos, Zephaniah, and the other prophets all speak of a future restoration of Israel.

God is always faithful to His word. He says there is a restoration, which has not happened; therefore, we can be confident that there is a restoration yet to occur.

## The New Testament Reiterates the Old Testament Expectation of Restoration of Israel

Romans chapters 9, 10, and 11 speak of Israel not as a "symbolic representation" of the church but a physical nation to which the Apostle Paul belongs:

> I tell the truth in Christ, I am not lying, my conscience also bearing me witness in the Holy Spirit, that I have great sorrow and continual grief in my heart. For I could wish that I myself were accursed from Christ for my brethren, my countrymen according to the flesh (Romans 9:1–3)

Paul is making it abundantly clear than any reference he makes to Israel in this discourse is not a symbolic reference to the church. He would be willing to be cut off from Christ for the sake of *his countrymen according to the flesh*.

Knowing he is speaking of the nation Israel, then, when we look at Romans 11, we get a glimpse of Israel's future.

> I say then, have they stumbled that they should fall? Certainly not! But through their fall, to provoke them to jealousy, salvation has come to the Gentiles. Now if their fall is riches for the world, and their failure riches for the Gentiles, how much more their fullness! (Romans 11:11–12)

The word used for "fall" in the initial question, "Have they stumbled that they should fall?" is the Greek word, *pipto*, which means to fall under judgement or come under condemnation. His question is literally, "Has Israel stumbled that they should be condemned?" Paul's answer is an emphatic, "Certainly not!" The Jewish nation has not been condemned, and so it cannot be said that God has rejected it.

He then explains how the Jews have "fallen" by using a different Greek word, *paraptoma*, which means to "slip up." The Jewish fall is described as a slipup. It has been a big slipup but a slipup all the same.

There is a coming national awakening in Israel.

> For if their being cast away is the reconciling of the world, what will their acceptance be but life from the dead? (Romans 11:15)

This verse describes a hardening of heart that has currently come on Israel, resulting in reconciliation for the Gentiles, but Paul says that their acceptance will be life from the dead. This is a promise of a national revival.

Jonathan Edwards, an eighteenth-century revivalist, said, "Nothing is more certainly foretold than this national conversion of the Jews in Romans 11."[29]

Charles H. Spurgeon said, "I think we do not attach sufficient importance to the restoration of the Jews. We do not think enough of it. But certainly, if there is anything promised in the Bible it is this."[30]

Theologian George E. Ladd says, "The New Testament clearly affirms the salvation of literal Israel."[31]

## The Old Testament Promises the Continual Survival of the Nation Israel

A plain reading of Jeremiah 31 shows the promise of Israel's continual survival.

> Thus says the Lord,
> Who gives the sun for a light by day,
> The ordinances of the moon and the stars for a light by night,
> Who disturbs the sea,
> And its waves roar
> (The Lord of hosts is His name):
> "If those ordinances depart
> From before Me, says the Lord,
> Then the seed of Israel shall also cease
> From being a nation before Me forever."
> Thus says the Lord:
> "If heaven above can be measured,
> And the foundations of the earth searched out beneath,
> I will also cast off all the seed of Israel
> For all that they have done, says the Lord."
> (Jeremiah 31:35–37)

The issue is paramount for all believers. If God promises that Israel will exist as long as there is a sun and a moon, along with all the stars in the sky, and then breaks the promise, how can we trust any of the promises of scripture?

> For all the promises of God in Him are Yes, and in Him Amen, to the glory of God through us.
> (2 Corinthians 1:2)

God promises to be faithful to keep all His promises. If He has broken this one promise to Israel, then He ceases to be trustworthy, faithful and absolute goodness and perfection. On the contrary, we believe that He will keep His promise to Israel and they remain His chosen people.

## Old Testament Promises and Covenants to Israel Are Still the Possession of Israel

Replacement Theology teaches that the covenants and the promises of the Old Testament are now the inheritance of the church, leaving Israel disinherited. The New Testament tells us something very different. Israel's promises and covenants are still theirs:

> "my kinsmen according to the flesh, who are Israelites, to whom belongs the adoption as sons and the glory and the covenants and the giving of the Law and the temple service and the promises" (Romans 9:3, 4)

This is not "spiritual Israel" or the church. Paul is speaking of is his kinsmen, according to the flesh, and he says to Israel "belongs the adoption as sons and the glory and the covenants and the giving of the Law and the temple service and the promises." Quite a list, but the key to all this the phase "to whom belongs," which shows those things listed are still in the possession of the Jews; otherwise, Paul would have said, "to whom *belonged* the adoption as sons and the glory and the covenants and the giving of the Law and the temple service and the promises."

What about Romans 9:6?
> But it is not that the word of God has taken no effect. For they are not all Israel who are of Israel. (Romans 9:6)

When Paul says, "For they are not all Israel who are of Israel," does that mean Israel has been replaced by a new Israel, the church? When Paul speaks of Israel, he is referring to his "kinsmen according to the flesh." Paul is not saying there is a spiritual Israel (i.e., the Christian Church) and a fleshly Israel, but rather within the nation of Israel there is a remnant that has embraced the Messiah and has inherited the promises of salvation. This is consistent with all other scriptures that talk of a remnant. The remnant was always "within" Israel, never Gentiles.

## The New Testament Indicates That God Is Faithful to Israel Because of His Promises to the Patriarchs of Israel

Israel's position is this: They have fallen (slipped) and are estranged for the benefit of Gentiles. However, this does not alter God's original choice of them. They are still the "apple of His eye," for the sake of the patriarchs.

> Concerning the gospel they are enemies for your sake, but concerning the election they are beloved for the sake of the fathers. (Romans 11:28)

The Abrahamic Covenant is still a covenant with Israel. Paul makes it clear he is not talking about the church but the natural descendants of Abraham.

> For I could wish that I myself were accursed from Christ for my brethren, my countrymen according to the flesh. (Romans 9:3)

Then he says:

> They are Israelites, and to them belong the adoption, the glory, the covenants, the giving of the law, the worship, and the promises. (Romans 9:4 ESV)

Israel still possesses all the promises and the covenants.

## Israel's Election/Calling Is Irrevocable

> For the gifts and the calling of God are irrevocable. (Romans 11:29)

Theologian Jürgen Moltmann says there is no doubt that Israel's place as God's chosen people has not changed.

> There can be no question of God's having finally rejected the people of his choice—he would then have to reject his own election (11.29) ... Israel's promises remain Israel's promises. They have not been transferred to the church. Nor does the church push Israel out of its place in the divine history. In the perspective of the gospel, Israel has by no means become 'like all the nations.'[32]

Another theologian, Wolfhart Pannenberg, makes this point: If Israel is no longer God's elect, then how is it possible to have confidence of our position in Christ?

> How could Christians be certain of their own comparatively new membership in the circle of God's elect if God for his part did not remain faithful to his election in spite of Israel's unbelief? This is the apostle's point when he advocates the inviolability of the election of the Jewish people (11:29; cf. 9:6). He has in mind also Christian assurance of election.[33]

## The New Testament Never Uses the Term "Israel" for Those Who Are Not Ethnic Jews

The name "Israel" appears seventy-three times in the New Testament. Each one of these references, with the possible exception of three, can only be interpreted as the people who are the natural descendants of Abraham, Isaac, and Jacob.

An objection could be made where Paul uses the phrase in Romans 11:26: "And all Israel will be saved." Another objection often used is Romans 9:6: "For they are not all Israel who are of Israel?" Does this indicate that all the nation of Israel will be saved with or without faith in Jesus? Is it a redefining of Israel to mean those of faith, the church? Or is it something different?

To answer these questions, we need to go back to Romans 9:1–5. Paul says that his heart breaks for Israel. She has a special place because God gave to her the covenants and the glory, the promises and the honour of service. What does it mean to have that special place yet reject the Messiah? Does it mean that the gospel is powerless and ineffective?

Of course not! Although the nation is descended from Abraham's seed, the children of God are the children of promise, but it is a remnant of the nation that is saved by grace—an Israel within Israel.

Then when Paul mentions Israel, he is not talking of a remnant but rather the nation:

> What shall we say then? That Gentiles, who did not pursue righteousness, have attained to righteousness, even the righteousness of faith; but Israel, pursuing the law of righteousness, has not attained to the law of righteousness. (Romans 9:30–31)

> But to Israel he says: "All day long I have stretched out My hands to a disobedient and contrary people." (Romans 10:21)

Each reference is to the nation, not to the church. All the descendants of Abraham, Isaac, and Jacob make up the nation, but only the remnant that pursue righteousness by faith in Yeshua are the children of God and referred to in Romans 11:26. The church has not replaced Israel.

## Replacement Theologians Fail to Show That the New Testament Reinterprets or Alters the Original Old Testament Prophecies regarding Israel

Paul quotes Jeremiah 31 when speaking of Israel, his "brethren according to the flesh," so one cannot claim that the Old Testament prophecies concerning Israel should be reinterpreted as referring to the church.

And so all Israel will be saved, as it is written:
"The Deliverer will come out of Zion,
And He will turn away ungodliness from Jacob;
For this is My covenant with them,
When I take away their sins." (Romans 11:26–27)

## New Testament Prophecies Refer to Israel, Thus Indicating That God's Plan for Israel Is Alive

In Revelation chapter 7, the prophecy speaks of the marking by God of 144,000. It then says that there are 12,000 from each of the tribes. This includes the ten lost tribes. How could we possibly see that as anything other than God still having a plan and a purpose for the nation of Israel?

Jesus' Olivet Discourse in Matthew 24 cannot be understood as anything other than a warning to Israel and a prophecy about Israel in the last days:

> "So when you see standing in the holy place 'the abomination that causes desolation,' spoken of through the prophet Daniel—let the reader understand— then let those who are in Judea flee to the mountains. Let no one on the housetop go down to take anything out of the house. Let no one in the field go back to get their cloak. How dreadful it will be in those days for pregnant women and nursing mothers! Pray that your flight will not take place in winter or on the Sabbath. For then there will be great distress, unequalled from the beginning of the world until now—and never to be equalled again. If those days had not been cut short, no one would survive, but for the sake of the elect those days will be shortened. At that time if anyone says to you, 'Look, here is the Messiah!' or, 'There he is!' do not believe it. For false messiahs and false prophets will appear and perform great signs and wonders to deceive, if possible, even the elect." (Matthew 24:15–24)

The fact we have end times prophecies in the New Testament that directly relate to, and only to, Israel, force us to conclude that God is not finished with the nation.

One startling observation is that Jesus will not return until the Jews, His chosen people, invite Him to come.

> See! Your house is left to you desolate; for I say to you, you shall see Me no more till you say, "Blessed is He who comes in the name of the Lord!" (Matthew 23:38–39)

Jesus is speaking to the Jewish leaders, not church leaders, saying that they will see Him only when Israel invites Him by acknowledging who He is and crying out, "Blessed is He who comes in the name of the Lord."

God still has a plan and a purpose for Israel.

## It Is Impossible for Replacement Theology to Explain Israel's Exile and Return

One of the great prophecies of the last days, and the key point of this book, is the exile and subsequent return of Israel into their own land. At the heart of Replacement Theology is the belief that because the nation rejected her Messiah, God has rejected her and replaced her with the church.

> I will be found by you, says the Lord, and I will bring you back from your captivity; I will gather you from all the nations and from all the places where I have driven you, says the Lord, and I will bring you to the place from which I cause you to be carried away captive. (Jeremiah 29:14)

> "'For behold, the days are coming,' says the Lord, 'that I will bring back from captivity My people Israel and Judah,' says the Lord. 'And I will cause them to return to the land that I gave to their fathers, and they shall possess it.'" (Jeremiah 30:3)

Who was exiled? Spiritual Israel, which is the church, or natural Israel, the nation? It can only be a reference to the nation of Israel. Who returned: spiritual Israel or natural Israel? Replacement theologians are obliged to say that the returning applies to the church because God is "finished with Israel." There are two reasons why this is absurd. Firstly, the church has never been exiled, so how can it return? Secondly, in the very same verse, you cannot change literal to figurative language; nor can you change the subject.

It can only be read thus: Israel is exiled and Israel returns, and that means that the church has never, nor will it ever, replace Israel.

## Conclusion

God is not finished with Israel. She still has a special place in God's heart, and He still has a plan and a purpose for the descendants of Abraham. Just as attending a church does not make an individual a Christian, in the same way that being born a Jew doesn't guarantee salvation. Individuals can be saved only by faith in Jesus, and in that sense, there is no Jew or Gentile. However, God still has a plan and a purpose for Israel as a nation. They remain God's chosen people. He still is in covenant with them because the sun came up this morning.

Israel remains one of the most hated nations on the planet, if not the most hated, and the church has been complicit in that hatred because of the heretical teaching that God has rejected His people.

In the next chapter, we will see why Israel is so hated.

# CHAPTER 4
## Esther—Anti-Semitism

*I know, I know. We are Your chosen people. But, once in a while, can't You choose someone else?*

—Tevye (from *Fiddler on the Roof*)

The Book of Esther is a book about God's protection and deliverance of a nation in the face of a disgraceful attempt at national genocide.

The story begins in Persia, when the king dismisses his queen for insubordination and then seeks to find another queen to replace her. The king chose Esther, a Jew. Following this Esther's cousin, Mordechai, overhears a plot to kill the king. Mordechai reports it, and the king is saved. Sometime later, the king's lieutenant, Haman, is offended by Mordechai and seeks to kill him. Haman devises a plan to hang Mordechai in the public square and kill all the Jews in Persia. But the plot fails. Not only are Mordechai and the Jews spared, but Mordechai is promoted to be the king's second in command, while Haman and his family are hanged on the very gallows he has assigned for Mordechai. Now every year the Jews celebrate this great deliverance during the feast of Purim.

Julius Streicher, one of ten Nazis sentenced to be hanged for war crimes in Nuremberg, on October 1, 1946, stared at the witnesses to his execution and shouted, "Purimfest, 1946." He obviously saw a link between his fate and the fate of Haman, some 2,500 years earlier.

The link has not been lost on Jews. When Haman was sentenced to death at the request of Esther, something significant happened. We read that the ten sons of Haman were hanged, but then in Esther 9:13, Esther makes a further request:

> "If it pleases the king, let it be granted to the Jews who are in Shushan to do again tomorrow according to today's decree, and let Haman's ten sons be hanged on the gallows."

Why hang the sons of Haman a second time?

The Hebrew word for "tomorrow" (*machar*) occasionally refers to the distant future and could mean that Esther is prophesying that the "ten sons of Haman" will hang again at some point in the distant future. Also in the list of Haman's sons, there are several unusually-sized letters. There is a large *vav* (numerical value = 6) and a small *tav* (400), *shin* (300), and *zayin* (7). The belief is that, in the sixth millennium, in the year 707 (400 + 300 + 7) Haman's sons would be hanged again. The year 5707 on the Jewish calendar corresponds to 1946.

This maybe a coincidence or an attempt to make scripture imply something it doesn't say, but I believe that "hang them again tomorrow" was prophetic and that the same spirit that drove Haman to attempt national genocide of the Jewish race is the same demonic spirit that drove the Nazis to attempt the same thing. I also believe it is the same spirit behind all anti-Semitic belief and action.

Even today, while talking peace, Arab leaders are plotting the annihilation of the Jews. The same as in the past.

Prior to the six-day war, Cairo Radio made these comments:

> May 19, 1967: "This is our chance Arabs, to deal Israel a mortal blow of annihilation, to blot out its entire presence in our holy land."[34]
>
> May 22, 1967: "The Arab people is firmly resolved to wipe Israel off the map."[35]

## Why the Hatred of the Jews?

No nation on the planet has suffered so much hate from so many people and for so long as the Jewish people. Why the hatred? Several reasons are given for anti-Semitic behaviour, but as we will see, they are simply excuses used to justify universal hatred of the Jews.

It need not be a difficult exercise to differentiate between a cause and an excuse.

Consider a car driver who is constantly being booked for speeding. He says the reason he speeds is that the odometer in his car is faulty. He has the odometer checked and calibrated, but again he is booked for speeding. The odometer was not the cause of his speeding; it was his excuse.

## The First "Cause" of Anti-Semitism Is Economic

Some make the argument that anti-Semitism is the result of the world's envy of Jewish wealth and power. If the cause of anti-Semitism is envy at the power and the wealth of Jews, why are impoverished Jews in the world also hated?

Jews who lived in the Jewish villages of Poland and Russia during the seventeenth to twentieth centuries were poor and powerless, utterly lacking any form of influence whatsoever, yet they too were hated and often massacred in cold blood.

Wealth and power of Jews is nothing more than an excuse; it is not the cause.

## The Second "Cause" of Anti-Semitism Is That They Don't Assimilate

Maybe Jews are hated simply because they are different.

Traditionally, Jews were characterised by different dress, laws, and even languages. Throughout history, Jews kept to themselves. Their ethical, cultural, and social systems were different from those of their neighbours, and their dream always was to return to Zion.

Is there a direct correlation between a reduction in anti-Semitism and an increase Jewish assimilation? When Jews begin adopting the culture of the surrounding society and seek to "fit in" better, do we see a reduction in the hatred? The answer is no.

In the eighteenth century, the Enlightenment reached Europe, giving equal rights to all people, regardless of religion. In December 1789, during a discussion in the French National Assembly in which French Jews were granted equal rights, Count Stanislas de Clermont-Tonnere declared, "We must refuse everything to the Jews as a nation and accord everything to Jews as individuals."[36] French Jews chose assimilation rather than isolation because they saw an opportunity to attain equality. They changed their appearance and attended universities and theatres. They adopted the language, culture, and styles of their non-Jewish neighbours and intermarried with them. They even ceased praying to return to the Promised Land. In a sense, they became more French than the French.

At the Synod of Reformed Rabbis held at Frankfurt in 1845, Rabbi Samuel Holdheim rejected the idea of a personal messiah and political redemption in the land of Israel.

> The hope for a national restoration contradicts our feeling for the fatherland. Messianic redemption in the Land of Israel contradicted loyalty to Germany as the fatherland. Therefore, the early Reformers rejected Jewish sovereignty in the Land of Israel out of fear of charges of dual loyalty. "Berlin is our Jerusalem!" was their clarion call.[37]

Did this end anti-Semitism? Those who thought it could were to be disappointed.

The Dreyfuss affair in the 1890s, in which falsified charges of treason were brought against a Jewish French officer, was contrived to show that Jews could never be loyal citizens of their host countries.

Shortly thereafter, Hitler's rise to power undermined the Jews' sense of security in their assimilationist approach. Nazism sent a strong message to Jews: We hate you not because you're different but because you're trying to become like us! We cannot allow you to infect the Aryan race with your inferior genes.

Anti-Semetic behaviour is not caused by the issues of assimilation; it is yet another excuse.

## The Third "Cause" of Anti-Semitism Is They Are an Inferior Race

This leads to another "cause": simply that the Jews are inferior.

You can change your appearance, you can seek to live "normal lives," and you can do as many did at the end of the nineteenth century, change your religion. But there is one thing you can never change, your race.

There is no distinguishing racial physical feature common only to Jews. Even the idea of a "Jewish nose" is a myth. Anti-Semites don't hate only those Jews who have distinctively Jewish physical features; they hate all Jews. They hate Eastern European Jews; they hate Israeli, Russian, and Yemenite Jews. They hate blond, blue-eyed Dutch Jews as well as dark-skinned Mediterranean Jews. Any Jew will do.

Anyone can become a Jew, and people have, from everywhere.

Anti-Semitism cannot be explained as racism. The Jews are a nation, not a race.

## The Forth "Cause" of Anti-Semitism is That They Arrogantly Claim to Be God's Chosen People

The forth "cause" is the arrogance of the Jews for believing they are "superior" because they are "God's chosen people." This contradicts the previous reason. How can one people be both inferior and yet superior? Hatred is not logical.

Again, what did Rabbi Samuel Holdheim say in Berlin in 1845? The Jews reject the idea of a personal messiah, and the hope for a national restoration contradicts our feeling for the fatherland. Berlin is our Jerusalem!

Where's the arrogance and the feelings of superiority in believing they are God's chosen people? It is not there, so did anti-Semitism disappear from

German society? Of course it didn't; instead of vanishing, the worst example of anti-Semitism manifested in less than one hundred years.

Again, what we have is an excuse, but we still seek a cause.

## The Fifth "Cause" of Anti-Semitism Is That They Are Responsible for Social and Economic Upheaval

The Jews have often been made the scapegoats for the ills of the world. Hitler, in his Nuremberg address, like many other totalitarian dictators, managed to divert blame for Germany's problems by ascribing them to the Jews.

The question must be, did Hitler randomly select the Jews as his scapegoat, or was it a well-thought-out plan? What if he addressed the crowds by saying this: "My fellow Germans, there is a group among us that is the scourge of humanity! They are dominating the German people and destroying our motherland! If Germany is to regain its esteemed status, these people must be persecuted and ultimately eliminated. Who are these people? They are the midgets among us!"

Would he have been able to get an entire nation to buy into the lie that midgets were to blame for Germany's problems? Of course not, so how did he get such national acceptance of the lie that the Jews were the problem? He had to connect with the nation, and to do so he tapped into a pre-existent hatred of the Jews.

This again is never the cause of anti-Semitism; it is another excuse. If there wasn't an almost universal hatred of the Jews, there would not have existed the opportunity to scapegoat the Jews.

## The Sixth "Cause" of Anti-Semitism Is Deicide (The Killers-of-Jesus Theory)

Christians have long claimed that the Jews killed Jesus and that is why they hate Jews. Is this the real cause for hatred?

If it is, why were Christians not angry at Jews two thousand years ago, at the time the Jews supposedly killed Jesus? If "deicide" is the cause of anti-Semitism, then how do we explain Haman and his desire to annihilate all the Jews five hundred years before Jesus' crucifixion? How can Antiochus Epiphanes' conduct be explained? Nearly two hundred years before Jesus' death, he stormed Jerusalem, killed thousands of Jews, and sold thousands more into slavery. The ultimate humiliation was the sacrifice of a pig on the altar of the temple in 167 BC.

What about the anti-Semitism amongst non-Christians? Christian anti-Semitism did not begin until long after the death of Jesus. It was not until several centuries later that the church fathers decided that Jews as a group should be persecuted because they "killed Jesus." In fact, Jews and Christians lived peaceably together for the first hundred years of the church, the time when the hatred should have been the most extreme.

So who killed Jesus? According to the New Testament, and in particular all four gospels, it was the Romans who killed Jesus, at the behest of the Jews. If the killing of Jesus is the cause of Christian hatred, why have only the Jewish accomplices been categorically persecuted? Christians should hate Italians at least as much as they hate Jews!

Obviously, Jesus' death is an excuse, not the reason for anti-Semitism.

If these are all excuses and not causes of anti-Semitism, is it possible to find the cause? If we do find the cause, then is hatred of the Jews their own fault?

## The Devil Hates the Abrahamic Covenant

We have seen six commonly held views as to why anti-Semitism has been rife in the world for thousands of years, but each of these must be an excuse. The real reason for anti-Semitism is that the devil hates what God loves.

God has chosen the descendants of Abraham, Isaac and Jacob as His special possession and so the devil has chosen them to be the object of his hate on earth.

> Who has made us Jews different from all other people? Who has allowed us to suffer so terribly up until now? It is God who has made us as we are, but it will be God, too, who will raise us up again. Who knows it might even be our religion from which the world and all peoples learn good, and for that reason and only that reason do we suffer. We can never become just Netherlanders, or just English or representatives of any country for that matter. We will always remain Jews, but we want to, too."[38]

—Anne Frank, *The Diary of a Young Girl*, April 11, 1944

Many people have a variety of reasons for why anti-Semitism is so rampant and universal in our world today. I believe this quote from Anne Frank's diary explains the root cause of anti-Semitism better than anything I have read: "Who knows it might even be our religion from which the world and all peoples learn good, and for that reason and only that reason do we suffer."

The classic *Fiddler of the Roof* tells the story of a small Jewish community in Russia. In one scene the main character, Tevye, says, "I know, I know. We are Your chosen people. But, once in a while, can't You choose someone else?"

God describes Israel as the "apple of His eye." One thing is true, what God loves, the devil hates; and the devil hates the covenant God made with His friend, Abraham.

The devil's hatred goes deeper than hating what God loves, his very survival depends on Israel. When man sinned, God made it clear that it was through a descendant of Adam that salvation would come. God said that enmity would be evident between the devil and the seed of the woman. The Bible is not just Israel's history but also God's redemption history.

Cain killed Abel, but why? The devil tried to thwart God's redemptive plan. The flood, caused by man's sin, would have seen redemption killed off if not for one man: Noah. God then chose Abraham, then Isaac, Jacob, and, centuries later, David.

The devil knew that the Messiah would be one of David's descendants. In 2 Kings 11, we read of how a wicked queen named Athaliah sought to destroy all David's descendants and came within one life of destroying God's redemption.

> When Athaliah the mother of Ahaziah saw that her son was dead, she arose and destroyed all the royal heirs. But Jehosheba, the daughter of King Joram, sister of Ahaziah, took Joash the son of Ahaziah, and stole him away from among the king's sons who were being murdered; and they hid him and his nurse in the bedroom, from Athaliah, so that he was not killed. So he was hidden with her in the house of the Lord for six years, while Athaliah reigned over the land. (2 Kings 11:1–3)

The Messiah has come. He defeated the devil at Calvary and will return. The devil is aware that the timing of Christ's return is tied to the nation of Israel, and when Jesus returns, he will be bound and thrown into the lake of fire. He knows his time is short.

> [T]he devil has come down to you, having great wrath, because he knows that he has a short time." (Revelation 12:12)

The devil knows that before Jesus returns to establish His kingdom in Jerusalem, the Jews need to be dwelling in Jerusalem, the eternal capital of the Jewish state. Chapter 13 shows that from Jerusalem the religious leaders will then invite Jesus to come.

The devil's tactic is simple: kill the Jews. He has tried and has been unsuccessful. So now his attention is on keeping the Jews out of Jerusalem, and that too has failed. His last hope is to keep their eyes blinded to the Messiah. To do that, over the centuries he has stirred up Christian hatred for the Jew in the hope that this will keep the Jews from acknowledging their Messiah. The truth is that too will fail. The Jewish nation will experience a spiritual awakening that will usher in the return of Jesus and the demise of the devil and his satanic hordes.

## Conclusion

In Genesis 15:11 we read that vultures came down on the carcasses but Abram drove them away. These vultures are a perfect representation of the enemies of Israel, who would seek to annihilate her. Abraham was driving them away until evening came. This is a sign that the covenant people would be delivered from the destruction threatened by their foes.

This is a perfect picture of the enemy's constant attempts to destroy God's covenant people. From Pharaoh in Exodus to Haman in Persia, and from Antiochus Epiphanes to Hitler's Nazis, they all had one thing in mind, the destruction of Israel and God's covenant with Abraham. At the end of the nineteenth century, the driving force in the rise of the Zionist Movement was rampant anti-Semitism, which led to the murder of Jews in a Russian village. The feeling was that the only safe haven was a Jewish homeland. Even in their own land, the day after Israel was declared a nation on, May 14, 1948, an Arab coalition of five states invaded Israel with the sole intention of destroying the nation.

Today, Hamas and Hezbollah, backed by Iran, constantly call for the complete destruction of Israel. One week before the 2015 parliamentary elections in Turkey, President Recep Tayyip Erdoğan called for the "liberation" of Jerusalem:

> Conquest is Mecca, conquest is Saladin, it's to hoist the Islamic flag over Jerusalem again.[39]

The vultures continue to circle Israel, but just as Abram fought them off in Genesis 15, Israel continues to fight off those that would destroy her. Each time her enemies have attacked since 1948, Israel has found herself in the end with more land.

# SECTION 2

# THE BONES ARE RATTLING (ISRAEL'S HOMECOMING)

# CHAPTER 5
## The Birth of a Nation

*The law of return is the law of enduring historical connection between our people and the land.*

—Prime Minister David Ben Gurion

One of the most well known Bible prophecies is found in Ezekiel 37. It also is one of the most misused scriptures by the church. Ezekiel sees a valley full of dead, dry bones. The bones are rattling and coming together. God tells the prophet that the bones represent the nation of Israel.[40] As we have seen, the church has a tendency to take prophecies about Israel's glorious future and apply them to the church. This section looks at the coming together of the nation of Israel as they return to their own land after nearly two thousand years of Exile.

Before the prophecy of bones could be fulfilled, Israel needed a land to return to. This chapter looks at the history of Israel in the decades preceding its declaration of Independence on May 14, 1948, a day that saw Isaiah's word in chapter 66 fulfilled.

> Before she was in labour, she gave birth;
> Before her pain came, she delivered a male child.
> Who has heard such a thing?
> Who has seen such things?
> Shall the earth be made to give birth in one day?
> Or shall a nation be born at once?
> For as soon as Zion was in labor,
> She gave birth to her children. (Isaiah 66:7–8)

We will look at the resolutions and agreements made (and reneged on) by governments in Europe and America. We also will examine whether there is any historic evidence to support Arab claims to Israel (Palestine) as their homeland.[41]

On November 29, 1947, the United Nations voted 33 for, 13 against, with 10 abstentions to establish the national homeland for the Jews. The nations that voted "Yes" included Australia and the United States. Significantly, one of the nations that abstained was Great Britain. As a nation, Great Britain originally strongly supported the Zionist dream for a Jewish homeland but continued to weaken her support and renege on many previous commitments.

Six months later, in a small hall in Tel Aviv, David Ben Gurion delivered the nation's "Proclamation of Independence" speech, and with these words the State of Israel was reborn:

> [M]embers of the People's Council, representatives of the Jewish Community of Eretz Yisrael[42] and of the Zionist Movement, are here assembled on the day of the termination of the British Mandate over Eretz Yisrael and, by virtue of our natural and historic right and on the strength of the resolution of the United Nations General Assembly, hereby declare the establishment of a Jewish state in Eretz Yisrael, to be known as the State of Israel.

All this seemed to happen in a day, but the reality was much different. The wheels of independence were turning even before the First World War.

The first *Aliyah* was from 1882 to 1903, when between 25,000 and 30,000 Jews migrated to Palestine as farmers.[43] However, many left the land after only a couple of years because of the harshness of their new life. A second *Aliyah*, from 1904 to 1914, saw a further 20,000 Jews return to Palestine. Among those returning was a nineteen-year-old from Poland named David Ben Gurion. These migrants were "idealists" looking for a Jewish homeland.

By the time Ben Gurion declared independence in 1948, there was more than 550,000 Jews living in the Promised Land. Among them were idealists like Ben Gurion, but most were escaping post war Europe.

## The Liberation of Jerusalem

In early 1917, during WWI, British and Allied troops were held back in the Sinai by the Turkish and German armies. The situation had become grave, and in the wake two failed attacks on Gaza and Beersheba the ANZACS and British troops were fast running out of water. The British War Office desperate for victory replaced the commander of the Egyptian Expeditionary Force, Sir Archibald Murray, with Sir Edmond Allenby. Allenby's appointment came with the commanded from the British Prime Minister, David Lloyd George, to "capture Jerusalem by Christmas."

By the end of October, the Allied forces had failed several more times to capture the key cities of Gaza and Beersheba. With the troops and horses out of water, disaster loomed large. On the afternoon of October 31, the Australian General Chauvel, commander of the Fourth and Twelfth Light Horse Brigades, came up with an audacious plan to charge the four thousand strong and heavily armed Turkish forces at Beersheba with just eight hundred Light Horsemen.

Miraculously, in less than an hour, Beersheba was captured and a military disaster was averted. The 3,500-year-old wells dug by Abraham were in British and Australian hands. Add to the miraculous victory, Beersheba, which has very low rainfall averages in October, had storms sweep over it the day before that filled the wells with ample water. With this attack, desperately needed water was accessed, and the Turkish defensive lines were breached. Australian, British, and New Zealand forces could now march on Jerusalem. This made Prime Minister Lloyd George's command to liberate Jerusalem by Christmas a real possibility.

A third miracle, at the same time the charge on Beersheba was taking place 3,600 kilometres away, the British War Cabinet was meeting in London. The last item on the agenda was how to deal with the "Zionist Movement." The discussion ended with the adoption of what become known as the "Balfour Declaration." It was this promise, which has been called "a scrap of paper that has changed the world," that led to the creation of the modern State of Israel. Israel was to be a nation in which all Jews would be free to return to, if they desired.

On November 2, three days after the War Cabinet's adoption of the Balfour Declaration, the Foreign Secretary, Lord Balfour, wrote to Lord Rothschild, a Jewish banker and politician and said, "His Majesty's Government view with favour the establishment in Palestine of a national home for the Jewish people."

Just six weeks later, on December 11, General Allenby walked through Jaffa gate, liberating Jerusalem from 1,300 years of Muslim rule. The last four hundred years under the Ottoman Caliphate, who I believe to be the eighth of Beast described in Revelation 13.[44]

Eleven months later, on November 11, 1918, WWI ended. The end of the war saw Palestine governed under a British Mandate for nearly thirty years.

As one war ended another began. Despite the Balfour Declaration, a new battle was now on in earnest, a battle to define what liberated Palestine was to look like, a battle that is still being waged today.

## Three More Binding Resolutions on Palestine

The Jews claimed a right to a homeland in Palestine because of the binding nature of the Balfour Declaration. However, three more resolutions would ensure the Jews' right to a homeland.

1. *The San Remo Resolution (April 24, 1920)*

In San Remo, Italy, the victorious Allied forces Britain, France, Japan, and Italy, with the United States attending as an observer, met to decide how the Middle East would look following the Ottoman rule. The final resolution of this meeting decided that, in time, the region would become the modern nations of Syria, Lebanon, Iraq and Palestine (Israel). Syria (founded in 1941) and Lebanon (1946) were initially under a French mandate, while Iraq (1932) and Israel (1948) were under British mandate.

There has been no debate, argument, or war fought over Syria, Lebanon, or Iraq's right to exist. Yet their borders and right to become modern nations were determined by the same resolution that confirmed Israel's right to exist. This is hypocritical and a clear double standard. If Israel's neighbours have a legal right to nationhood, then so too does Israel.

Regarding Palestine, the San Remo Resolution stated,

> The High Contracting Parties agree to entrust ... the administration of Palestine, within such boundaries as may be determined by the Principal Allied Powers, to a Mandatory [authority that] will be responsible for putting into effect the [Balfour] declaration ... in favour of the establishment in Palestine of a national home for the Jewish people.[45]

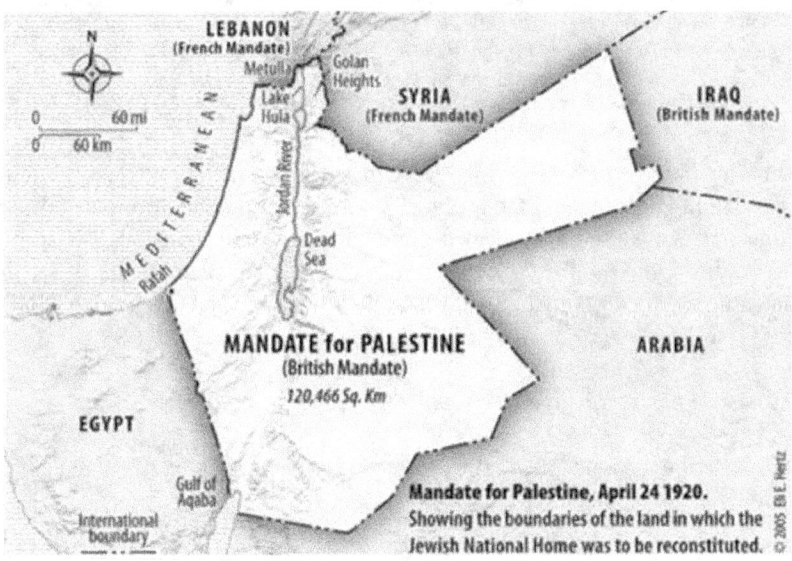

Figure 1 - Mandate for Palestine April 24, 1920

The San Remo Resolution determined the borders of Palestine. According to the resolution and the Balfour Declaration, within Palestine there was to be a homeland for the Jews. On a modern map, the borders of mandated Palestine, the Jewish homeland, includes Gaza and the West Bank (Palestinian enclaves), Israel (as it is known today), and Jordan to the East.

The Arabs living in Palestine at the time objected, and within three months, the British, after consultation with the high commissioner for Palestine, Sir Herbert Samuel, reduced the determined boundaries and Churchill redefined what "in Palestine" meant in his White Paper dated June 3, 1921.[46]

> [T]he terms of the Declaration referred to do not contemplate that Palestine as a whole should be converted into a Jewish National Home, but that such a Home should be founded "in Palestine."[47]

This was never the intention of the Balfour Declaration. In the book *Israel, the West Bank, and International Law*, Allan Gerson noted,

> The field in which the Jewish National Home was to be established was understood, at the time of the Balfour Declaration, to be the whole of historic Palestine and the Zionists were seriously disappointed when Trans-Jordan was cut away from the field under Article 25. This was done ... in obedience to the McMahon Pledge[48] which was antecedent to the Balfour Declaration.[49]

This first act of appeasement by Britain led to a dramatic change in Jewish aspirations in Palestine and the loss of 75 per cent of the land promised through Balfour and San Remo. This was a dramatic and disadvantageous decision for the Jews, but *it did reaffirm their right to an independent Jewish state.* The Jews reluctantly accepted the reduction of land, but the Arabs, who benefited from the changes, still protested, and they did so violently.

2. *The Mandate for Palestine (July 24, 1922)*

In 1922, the League of Nations passed a resolution creating the Palestine Mandate, which included the following clause:

> Whereas recognition has thereby been given to the historical connection of the Jewish people with Palestine and to the grounds for reconstituting their national home in that country.[50]

This resolution clearly acknowledged the Jews have a historic connection to the region called Palestine. What was equally noteworthy is that no such recognition of a similar Arab connection was mentioned.

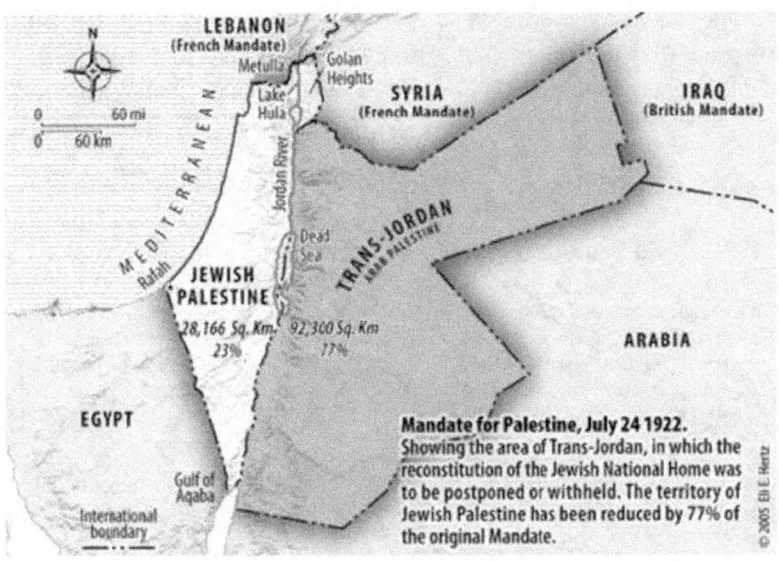

Figure 2 - Mandate for Palestine July 24, 1922

3. *Anglo-American Convention on Palestine (December 5, 1924)*

Israel's right to a homeland in Palestine, initially stated in the Balfour Declaration, confirmed in both the San Remo and the League of Nations mandates, was further strengthened by the 1924 "Anglo-American Convention on Palestine," which stated,

> Whereas the Principal Allied Powers have also agreed that the Mandatory should be responsible for putting into effect the declaration originally made on the 2$^{nd}$ of November 1917, by the Government of His Britannic Majesty, and adopted by the said Powers, in favour of the establishment in Palestine of a national home for the Jewish people.[51]

It is my belief that the Jewish people are the sole beneficiaries of self-determination in the land that was Mandatory Palestine. The rights of the Jewish people to all of Palestine are enshrined in these three legally binding international treaties. These rights have never been negated.

## Three More Mandates to a Homeland

The Jews have unquestionable legal and binding right to an independent state in Palestine. However, Jews would also claim their rights do not end with these legal documents and rulings. They could justifiably cite three other reasons for a Jewish homeland.

1. *A Biblical Mandate*

In 1971, David Ben Gurion gave his last public speech, in which he said,

> In the Declaration [of Independence] ... the Jews' right to return to the land is deemed to have preceded the founding of the state. The source of this right is the historic bond, never broken, between the Jews and their ancient land. The Law of Return is the law of the enduring historical connection between our people and the land, and it spells out the political principle under which the State of Israel was brought to life?[52]

What is this historic bond that has never been broken? It is the covenant that God made with Abraham.

> Now the Lord had said to Abram:
> "Get out of your country,
> From your family
> And from your father's house,
> To a land that I will show you.
> I will make you a great nation;
> I will bless you
> And make your name great;
> And you shall be a blessing.
> I will bless those who bless you,
> And I will curse him who curses you;
> And in you all the families of the earth shall be blessed." (Genesis 12:1–3)

This covenant was then confirmed in Isaac, not Ishmael.

> But My covenant I will establish with Isaac, whom Sarah shall bear to you at this set time next year." (Genesis 17:21)

> Then the Lord appeared to him [Isaac] and said: "Do not go down to Egypt; live in the land of

which I shall tell you. Dwell in this land, and I will be with you and bless you; for to you and your descendants I give all these lands, and I will perform the oath which I swore to Abraham your father. And I will make your descendants multiply as the stars of heaven; I will give to your descendants all these lands; and in your seed all the nations of the earth shall be blessed. (Genesis 26:2–4)

And then it was made to Jacob (Israel) and not Esau.

And behold, the Lord stood above it and said: "I am the Lord God of Abraham your father and the God of Isaac; the land on which you lie I will give to you and your descendants. Also your descendants shall be as the dust of the earth; you shall spread abroad to the west and the east, to the north and the south; and in you and in your seed all the families of the earth shall be blessed. (Genesis 28:13–14)

The covenant promises Abraham would father a great nation and that nation would be established through his son, Isaac, and grandson, Jacob. Abraham had more than one son, but God chose Isaac. Likewise, Isaac had two sons, but God chose the Jacob.

Secondly, the promise to Abraham involved land, "The Promised Land." God told Abraham, "Go to the land I show you," and to Isaac He said, "Dwell in this land," and to Jacob, "the land on which you lie I will give to you and your descendants." This is the *historic bond* to which Ben Gurion referred.

Several times Israel has been forced from the land because of sin and rebellion. God promised that exile was never permanent and He would bring them home to their land.

There is a clear historic bond between the land and the Jews, but what about the Arabs and the land? Is there a similar or even stronger bond? All the resolutions discussed acknowledged the bond between Jew and land. Not one ever acknowledged a similar Arab bond to land. Is this an oversight, discrimination, or simply a lack of Arab historic bond in existence?

Muhammad Al-Hussaini, a fellow and lecturer in Islamic studies at Leo Baeck Rabbinical College, London, says,

Until now, there has been no proper dialogue about these founding texts. But a dialogue is possible, first by recognizing that the Qur'an does, in fact, confirm the Biblical promise, then by re-reading commentaries on the Qur'anic text where the Jewish claim is strengthened. Beyond that, although the Jews come in for severe criticism in the works of Muslim apologists and theologians, there are no grounds in religious law to entertain the conceit that God's promise to the Children of Israel has been broken, and none to support the view that Israel is now the property of the Muslims.[53]

The Jordanian Quranic scholar Sheikh Ahmad al-Adwan, also called the "Zionist Sheikh," claims that according to the Quran, the land of Israel is promised to the Jews. He wrote,

> Indeed, I recognize their sovereignty over their land. I believe in the Holy Koran, and this fact is stated many times in the book. For instance, 'O my people! Enter the holy land which Allah hath assigned unto you,' [Koran 5:21], 'We made the Children of Israel inheritors of such things.' [Koran 26:59] and additional verses in the Holy Book.[54]

Coupled with this, Kuwaiti writer Abdullah Saad Al-Hadlaq urges for normal diplomatic relations with Israel. Al-Hadlaq argues that the Holy Quran emphasises the right of 'Bani Israel to Jerusalem.[55,56]

Abdul Hadi Palazzi, secretary general of the Italian Muslim Assembly and the Khalifah for Europe of the Qadiri Sufi Order, believes that

> [w]hile the reality of the Jewish people is a known fact, the idea of the Palestinian people is something that was created recently for political reasons. We easily admit a system of an Arab people but claiming that those Arabs who live inside Israeli territory are Palestinians and that they therefore have specific nationality is something that has no ethnic or historic basis.[57]

He firmly believes that the Quran itself makes it clear that the "Promised Land" was promised to the Jews, not the Arabs:

> And [mention, O Muhammad], when Moses said to his people, "O my people, remember the favour of Allah upon you when He appointed among you prophets and made you possessors and gave you that which He had not given anyone among the worlds. O my people, enter the Holy Land which Allah has assigned to you and do not turn back [from fighting in Allah's cause] and [thus] become losers."[58]

Not only does Palazzi believe that the Quran says the Holy (Promised) Land belongs to the Jews, but he also says that in the last days the Jews would return there:

> And We said after Pharaoh to the Children of Israel, "Dwell in the land, and when there comes the promise of the Hereafter, we will bring you forth in [one] gathering."[59]

It was reported in the Jewish press on May 7, 2012, that the Hamas minister of interior and national security, Fathi Hammad, said that Palestinians came from Egypt, Yemen, and Saudi Arabia. He said that all Palestinians have Arab roots and blood ties in various countries on the Arabian Peninsula and in Egypt. He also stated that half his family was Egyptian and over thirty large families are named Al-Matzri, originating from Egypt. Half of all Gazans came from Egypt; the other half came from Saudi Arabia and Yemen. He repeated and clarified this by asking,

> Who are the Palestinians? We have many families named Al-Matzri, whose roots are Egyptian. Egyptians! They came from Alexandria, Cairo, Dumietta, the North, from Aswan and Upper Egypt. We are Egyptians. We are Arabs. We are Muslims. We are a part of you.

As if to press his point, he added,

> We all have Arab roots, and every Palestinian, in Gaza and throughout Palestine, can prove his Arab roots—whether from Saudi Arabia, from Yemen, or anywhere. We have blood ties. So where is your affection and mercy?[60]

In addition, the Palestine Liberation Organisation (PLO), a terrorist group, was not the creation of Palestinians but rather the creation of the Arab League.[61] Its founding chairman was Ahmad Shukeiri who was born in the Lebanese town of Tebnine. He was replaced as chairman by an Egyptian, Yassar Arafat, who was born on August 4, 1929, in Cairo, and died on November 11, 2004, in Clamart, France.

While it appears the emergence of a national psyche amongst the Arabs living in Palestine was a product of last century, some want to push that date back. Some argue that this dates to an Arab revolt in 1834. Others argue for an even earlier date, in the seventeenth century. What is clear is that a Jewish historic bond dates back four millennia, all the way back to the Patriarchs, whereas a Palestinian bond, if one even exists at all, dates back, at most, to two or three centuries.

It is the Jews, and not the Arabs, who have a Biblical and historic connection to the Land.

## 2. *An Economic Mandate*

While there is a legal right and a historic connection, it is also argued that the Jews have an economic connection to the Land of Israel.

As we have seen earlier in the chapter, during the nineteenth century, the Jews began returning in greater numbers to their "Promised Land." As early as the mid-1850s, well before the first *Aliyah*, Jews were attempting to live productively in Ottoman Palestine. They began to buy land that had been terribly neglected at highly inflated prices and set about building villages called *moshavot*.[62] Sir Moses Montefiore made the first known land purchase, 10 hectares of orange groves in Jaffa. Other private acquisitions followed, and by 1882, some 2,200 hectares had been purchased by Jews.

The migrants began to drain swamps, clear stones, and developed techniques to prevent soil erosion. As Michael Rydelnik describes it,

> When Zionist Jewish settlers returned they found the land to be denuded of trees with its corollary loss of topsoil. The northern part of the land was swamp-laden due to clogging of rivers. The cities and towns were in ruins and disease was rampant.
>
> The biblical land of milk and honey, noted for its great fertility, was now a wasteland.[63]

It was true to say that biblical land of milk and honey, renowned for being fertile, was in fact a veritable wasteland. Rydelnik continues,

> By planting trees, irrigating barren areas, and draining swamps, returning Jewish settlers began industry and farm exports. The Jewish people reclaimed their forsaken land with their own blood and sweat, making it productive once again. Working a land that was no longer economically viable, Israel claims that Jewish commitment to the land caused an economic rebirth. As a result, Arabs from surrounding areas moved to Palestine to share in the wealth created by the Jewish economic revival.[64]

As the land became fruitful again, both Jewish and Arab migration increased. In the hundred years prior to the British Mandate, the population of Palestine increase by around 500,000. The non-Jewish population increased by 60 per cent, from 268,100 to 673,300, while the Jewish population increased by 70 per cent, from 24,000 to 83,800. This dramatic increase in population placed stress on the land and led to claims from Arabs that there were too many Jews migrating to Palestine. In 1937, the Peel Commission found otherwise:

> The shortage of land is due less to purchase by Jews than to the increase in the Arab population. The Arab claims that the Jews have obtained too large a proportion of good land cannot be maintained. Much of the land now carrying orange groves was sand dunes or swamps and uncultivated when it was bought[65]

In fact, the Peel Commission found that the Arab population was better off because the Jews were farming the land:

"Up till now the Arab cultivator has benefited on the whole both from the work of the British Administration and the presence of Jews in the country." [66]

The conclusion from Peel Commission Report is clear-cut: the shortage of land in Palestine was caused by an increase in the Arab population. Why the massive increase in the Arab population? As the Jewish migrants worked to reclaim the land, which had suffered from decades of neglect under Turkish rule, the land became more productive and migration increased, resulting in perceived overpopulation.

Peel said that overpopulation was an Arab problem. However, the British, in yet another attempt to placate the Arab majority, sought to limit the migration of Jews to the very region where they were to establish a Jewish homeland. All the while, the British refused to place similar restrictions on Arab migration.

Arabs began to complain that the "best and most fertile" parts of Palestine were being given to Israel. That is simply wrong. Not only did Israel repair centuries of neglect and turn a wasteland in an oasis, but Israel had not been awarded any land.

In 1947, the United Nations proposed a division of the land. Israel agreed to this proposal and declared independence. On the other hand, believing that they could win a quick and decisive victory, the Arabs never agreed to the UN Resolution 181. In response, the nations surrounding the newly independent Israel invaded. After this war of Independence in 1948–49 the land occupied by Israel became Israel, and the land occupied by the Arabs was known as Palestine. Consequently, it is the 1949 armistice lines, not UN Resolution 181, that is recognised by most as Israel's borders.

Israel can rightly claim to have an "economic mandate" to the land because much of Israel's territory in 1947 was incapable of producing crops until she developed revolutionary land cultivation techniques that saw the desert become fertile again. Israel has turned the economy around and has the right to enjoy the fruits of their labour.

We will look in more depth at the transformation of the Land of Israel in chapter 11.

### 3. *Human Rights Mandate*

Finally, it is my strong conviction Israel has a clear human rights mandate to live peacefully in the Land of Israel. Whenever human rights is mentioned, for some bizarre reason, it is always about Israel's "treatment" of the Arabs. Not for a moment does anyone consider Arabs' human rights abuses aimed at Israel. For example, in 2015-16, the UN adopted twenty-three resolutions criticising nations for their behaviour. Of the twenty-three resolutions, one was critical of Iran and the restrictions it places on individual freedoms, one critical of Syria for human rights abuses, and likewise one on North Korea for human rights abuses. The other twenty were all critical of Israel.[67]

There were twenty resolutions condemning Israel and just one for each of the *Axis of Evil* nations, so-named by the former President of the United States George W Bush. This is yet another example of bias against Israel.

UN bias can also be seen in an extraordinary event from 1952. In that year, there was an Israeli initiative at the UN to bring about a ceasefire in Korea. This initiative encountered serious opposition and was only passed once Norway replaced Israel as the sponsor of the resolution. Under Israel's leadership, the resolution was rejected. The same resolution under Norway passed easily.[68]

Israel's UN ambassador, Abba Eban would later quip, "If Algeria introduced a resolution declaring that the earth was flat and that Israel had flattened it, it would pass by a vote of 164 to 13 with 26 abstentions."[69]

Here is a just two examples of those twenty resolutions:

> [UN] deplores those policies and practices of Israel that violate the human rights of the Palestinian people and other Arabs of the occupied territories.[70]

> [UN is] expressing grave concern about the continuing systematic violation of the human rights of the Palestinian people by Israel, the occupying Power.[71]

Both of these are highly critical of Israel and their "treatment" of Arabs living in the *occupied territories* of the Gaza Strip, the West Bank, and the Golan Heights. But the question no one asks is why were they occupied? The question is never asked because the world knows and hates the answer. These regions are occupied because the Arabs, led by Egypt, Jordan, and Syria, invaded Israel with the intent of annihilating her. Had Israel been left in peace, there would be no occupied territories as defined by the UN.

In his independence speech, Prime Minister Ben Gurion made an impassioned appeal to the United Nations:

> We appeal to the United Nations to assist the Jewish people in the building-up of its State and to receive the State of Israel into the community of nations.[72]

He then went on to make this appeal to the Arabs living in both Israel and the surrounding nations:

> We appeal—in the very midst of the onslaught launched against us now for months—to the Arab inhabitants of the State of Israel to preserve peace and participate in the upbuilding of the State on the basis of full and equal citizenship and due representation in all its provisional and permanent institutions.
>
> We extend our hand to all neighbouring states and their peoples in an offer of peace and good neighbourliness, and appeal to them to establish bonds of cooperation and mutual help with the sovereign Jewish people settled in its own land. The State of Israel is prepared to do its share in a common effort for the advancement of the entire Middle East.[73]

Ben Gurion offered an olive branch to the Arabs, but what was their response? Let the Azzam Pasha (secretary general of the Arab League 1945–1952) answer for us. On the day Israel declared its independence, at a Cairo press conference, Pasha was reported as saying, "This will be a war of extermination and a momentous massacre which will be spoken of like the Mongolian massacres and the Crusades."[74]

Almost immediately, five Arab nations with whom Israel shares common borders—Egypt, Jordan, Syria, and Lebanon, along with Iraq—invaded the fledgling nation. While the Jews offered an olive branch, the Arab nations responded with war. Ben Gurion offered full and equal citizenship and due representation at all levels of government, while the Arabs swore annihilation. We examine Israel democracy, which embraces Arabs as well as Jews, in chapter 9.

The Independence War was not the end of the matter. Since 1949, Israel has been involved in a further seven wars and five military operations. In 1967, Israel was involved in a war with Egypt, Syria, Jordan, and Iraq, known as the Six-Day War. Arabs used the usual hate-filled rhetoric in the months leading up to the war.

> The existence of Israel is an error which must be rectified. This is our opportunity to wipe out the ignominy which has been with us since 1948. Our goal is clear—to wipe Israel off the map.
>
> —President Aref of Iraq[75]

> All Egypt is now prepared to plunge into total war which will put an end to Israel.
>
> —Cairo Radio[76]

Ahmed Shukairy, chairman of PLO in East (Jordanian) Jerusalem, was asked in a news interview, "What will happen to the Israelis if there is a war?" He responded, "Those who survive will remain in Palestine. I estimate that none of them will survive."[77]

In the escalating tensions prior to the war, British Prime Minister Harold Wilson summed it up perfectly:

> The characteristic of this situation is the declared aim of one side not to win concessions from the other. Their demand is that Israel should cease to exist—indeed has never existed ... What had to be sought was not merely how to avoid war but to create the conditions of peace. One condition of a lasting peace must be the recognition that Israel has a right to live. Israel had been for nearly 20 years a member of the United Nations entitled to the respect and protection of the United Nations."[78]

Every war involving Israel, except for the Suez Crisis (October 1956), was instigated by Arab nations. The Suez Crisis was an alliance of three nations—Britain, France, and Israel—whose goal was to reopen the Suez Canal, which had been blockaded by Egypt. Following that victory, Israel returned all the Egyptian land occupied during the conflict.

Throughout his public life, Ben Gurion never deviated from the belief that every person in Israel is equal. In his last public address, he again forcefully declared that everyone in Israel is equal irrespective of religion and ethnicity.

> In Israel proper no preference is accorded Jewish citizens over Arab citizens or other non-Jewish citizens. The Declaration of Independence affirms that "The State of Israel will maintain complete equality of social and political rights for all its citizens, without regard to religion, race or sex.[79]

This can hardly be defined as a human rights violation. It is more than just inaccurate, it is a blatant lie to say that Israel, and not the Arabs are the aggressors in the Middle East. In the words of Hamas leader Mahmoud a-Zahar, "Hamas must lay the foundation for a tomorrow without Zionists."[80] Iran's former president Mahmoud Ahmadinejad has made many statements declaring that Israel should be "wiped off the map."[81]

The Anti-Defamation League says,

> Israel is committed to pursuing a negotiated peace agreement with the Palestinians so that it may finally live in peace and security. Israel was able to reach historic peace agreements with

Egypt (1979) and Jordan (1994) in which both sides made serious compromises for the sake of normalized relations.

While Israel has made great efforts to promote serious negotiations and a final peace agreement with the Palestinians over the past two decades, peace has proved elusive primarily because there has not been a Palestinian peace partner willing to recognize Israel's right to exist as a Jewish state and able to uphold peace commitments.[82]

The truth is that Israel has remained steadfast in its desire for peace, while the Arabs have remained equally steadfast in their desire to annihilate the Jews. While sponsoring UN resolutions against Israel, the Arabs in Israel refuse to negotiate for peace and have instigated the wars in Israel since its birth.

These wars are a violation of Israel's human rights. Yet the greatest human rights violation is rampant anti-Semitism. As discussed previously, in chapter 4, anti-Semitism has raged from Bible times right up to this day: from the Pagan nations of the Bible to the Roman and Ottoman Empires, from Christians and Muslims alike. It seems everyone hates the Jews.

In the eighteenth century, as we came into the time of "enlightenment" and religious influence began to wane, Judaism was attacked as an outdated belief system that stifled human progress. Nineteenth-century Europe saw Jews as outsiders and subjected them to increased hatred and deadly persecution. In 1881–1882, the Tzar of Russia sponsored a huge wave of pogroms, violent attacks on Jewish communities, in the Russian Empire. Consequently, a massive wave of Jews began leaving, and Zionism, the desire for a homeland, was born.

The Balfour Declaration was the result of a desire for Jews to live in safety, away from rampant anti-Semitism. Today, Israel remains one the most maligned nations on earth. The constant attacks on Jews for no other reason than they are Jews is a flagrant human rights abuse and is yet another reason for the need of a Jewish home.

## What of Jerusalem?

For the thirty years from the Balfour Declaration to the adoption of Resolution 181 at the UN, there were many commissions and enquiries aimed at placating the Arabs. Every enquiry sought to reduce the size of the nation of Israel to appease them. From the original agreement, Churchill's white paper divided Palestine into Jewish Palestine (all land west of the Jordan) and Arab Palestine (Jordan), thus taking 77 per cent of the land promised to Israel and giving it the Arabs. Then in 1947, UN Resolution 181 took the remaining 25 per cent of

Israel and divided it again, giving a further 43 per cent of Israel to the Arabs. The UN also decided that Jerusalem would be a "separated body" and placed under an international regime and conferred upon it a special status due to its shared religious importance.

Cambridge Professor Sir Elihu Lauterpacht, judge *ad hoc* of the International Court of Justice and a renowned editor of *International Law Reports*, said,

> Not only are the two problems separate; they are also quite distinct in nature from one another. So far as the Holy Places are concerned, the question is for the most part one of assuring respect for the existing interests of the three religions and of providing the necessary guarantees of freedom of access, worship, and religious administration [E. H., as mandated in Article 13 and 14 of the "Mandate for Palestine"] ... As far as the City of Jerusalem itself is concerned, the question is one of establishing an effective administration of the City which can protect the rights of the various elements of its permanent population—Christian, Arab and Jewish—and ensure the governmental stability and physical security which are essential requirements for the city of the Holy Places.
>
> Nothing was said in the Mandate about the internationalization of Jerusalem. Indeed, Jerusalem as such is not mentioned—though the Holy Places are. And this in itself is a fact of relevance now. For it shows that in 1922 there was no inclination to identify the question of the Holy Places with that of the internationalization of Jerusalem.[83]

The notion of internationalising Jerusalem was never part of the original "mandate." It was always the intent of Britain under Balfour, the white paper, and the League of Nations that Jerusalem was to be wholly part of Jewish-Palestine, while recognising and respecting the connection of Christians and Muslims to Jerusalem.

Despite this, to placate the Arab population, the UN chose to place Jerusalem under an international regime. Israel, although losing out regarding both the size of their nation and Jerusalem accepted the conditions. By their acceptance, the Jews surrendered control of their spiritual, political, and historical capital, while the Arabs declared war.

Following the 1948 Arab-Israeli War, the Old City (East Jerusalem) was captured by Jordan and all its Jewish residents were exiled. West Jerusalem was under Israeli control. This remained the case for twenty years.

On June 7, 1967, Israeli Defence Forces liberated Jerusalem's Old City and the Western Wall, which was subsequently annexed as Israeli territory. For the first time since 135 CE, when Hadrian's army defeated the Jews, renamed Jerusalem Aelia Capitolina, and banned Jews from living there, the Old City of Jerusalem was in Jewish hands. What the Balfour Declaration says, and what San Remo, along with the League of Nations and International Law, confirms—but the UN chooses to ignore and Arabs outright reject—is that Jerusalem belongs to Israel and is now rightfully in Israel's possession.

Israel will not surrender control of Jerusalem, and nor should she. Today an undivided Jerusalem is Israel's capital.

## Conclusion

Israel was born on May 15, 1948. Her birth is legitimate and enshrined in international law. There is a Biblical mandate going back to the Patriarchs and an economic mandate arising from the way the Jews replenished the land, resulting in a now-thriving Western economy. Not bad for a nation of 6 million in a land of 22,000 km$^2$. There is also a human rights mandate. She is the only combatant seeking peace, and historical and contemporary anti-Semitism necessitates a homeland as a human-rights issue.

As for Jerusalem, despite UN Resolution 181, international law says Jerusalem belongs to Israel, and since 1967, Jerusalem has remained the undivided capital of Israel. And so it should remain.

In chapters 6 and 7, we study the return of Israelis to their newly formed nation despite the ongoing battle over Israel's right to a homeland. Led by Arabs and supported by the United Nations, Israel is still being pressured by the international community to give land for peace. In chapter 8, we will look the effort to divide Israel and what God's response will be to those efforts.

# CHAPTER 6
## Ezekiel—A Nation of Dry Bones

*The prophecies of Ezekiel 37 have been fulfilled.*

—Prime Minister Benjamin Netanyahu

In the years leading up to and following the momentous events of 1947, when the UN passed the Resolution 181, paving the way for a Jewish homeland and Israel's declaration of Independence in 1948, we saw an acceleration in the fulfilment of Ezekiel's prophecy. At the end of World War 2, there were just 550,000 Jews living in Palestine, but by 1958, ten years after independence, Israel's population had grown to 2,032,000.[84] Hitler designed a plan to exterminate an entire race, but God used that evil scheme to expedite His plan and bring His covenant people home. In this chapter, we will look at the effect of anti-Semitism, particularly the holocaust and how it resulted in such a massive migration of Jews to *Eretz Yisrael*.

The return of Jews from all over the world and principally Europe was not accompanied by a tickertape parade. The returning Jews were dishevelled, persecuted and poor.

Due to sustained anti-Semitism, Jews were returning to their homeland long before Israel was liberated from Muslim rule. This return, known as *Aliyah*,[85] occurred in five waves. What had begun in the nineteenth century with the first *Aliyah* would gain a massive boost in momentum as persecution increased. The table below shows that the fifth *Aliyah* saw nearly a quarter of million Jews flood back to Palestine in the ten years that led to the holocaust.

| Aliyah | Years | Number of Jewish Immigrants | From |
|---|---|---|---|
| 1st | 1882–1903 | 25,000–35,000 (Up to 90% left again) | Russian, Yemen |
| 2nd | 1904–1914 | 40,000 | Russia |
| 3rd | 1919–1923 | 40,000 | Eastern Europe |
| 4th | 1924–1929 | 82,000 | Poland, Hungary |

| 5th | 1929–1939 | 250,000 | Germany |

Table 6.1 - Migrants in each Alijah

As we have seen, in the years following the WWII, Israel's fast-growing population passed the 2 million mark.

The fifth *Aliyah*, which saw 250,000 Jews leave Germany in the 1930s, coincided with Hitler's rise to power, and all the persecution that had gone before was about to go to whole new level with the Nazis' plan to murder 11 million European Jews. The audacious and evil plan, written on a napkin over a cup of tea one Sunday afternoon, would see the extermination of an entire race. Country by country the Nazis wrote down the number of Jews to be murdered, 11 million in total.

When the Auschwitz death camp was liberated on January 27, 1945, the sight that met the Russian troops was simply horrific. The remaining 7,000 Jews were nothing more than skin and bones. It would have seemed like the valley of dry bones that Ezekiel prophesied about.

This has never lost on the psyche of Jews everywhere. Israeli Prime Minister Benjamin Netanyahu, in a speech commemorating the sixty-fifth anniversary of liberation of Auschwitz, on the actual site of the Nazi death camp, declared that Ezekiel 37 has been fulfilled.[86]

> The hand of the Lord came upon me and brought me out in the Spirit of the Lord, and set me down in the midst of the valley; and it was full of bones. Then He caused me to pass by them all around, and behold, there were very many in the open valley; and indeed they were very dry. And He said to me, "Son of man, can these bones live?" So I answered, "O Lord God, You know." (Ezekiel 37:1–3)

In answer to God's question, can these bones live? How could Ezekiel have said, "Yes, for sure"? Likewise, after seeing these 7,000 Jews in Germany's death camps, how could anyone envisage what would follow? If not for the hand of God coming upon them and miraculously raising them up, Jewish prosperity would be difficult, if not impossible, to envisage.

God then tells Ezekiel to prophesy to the bones.

> Again He said to me, "Prophesy to these bones, and say to them, 'O dry bones, hear the word of the Lord! Thus says the Lord God to these bones: "Surely I will cause breath to enter into you, and you shall live. I will put sinews on you and bring flesh upon you, cover you with skin and put breath in you; and you shall live. Then you shall know that I am the Lord."'"

> So I prophesied as I was commanded; and as I prophesied, there was a noise, and suddenly a rattling; and the bones came together, bone to bone. (Ezekiel 37:4–7)

What Ezekiel saw and Netanyahu declared as the fulfilment of prophecy was the greatest miracle of the twentieth century. The Jews were coming home to their own land.

## Worse Than It Should Have Been

Some people, including Pat Buchanan, who served as a senior advisor to three American presidents, say the Holocaust was avoidable, which is debatable; however, more should have been done to minimise its impact. Hitler from the outset was a rabid anti-Semite, and more should have been done earlier to minimise his influence. With Hitler's rise power in 1933, Jews sought to leave Germany *en masse*. The sad fact is that no nation was willing to accept these Jewish refugees.

Despite British and international promises of a Jewish homeland in Palestine,[87] their policies were designed to appease the Arabs, and Palestine's borders remained closed to Germany's Jews. Hundreds of thousands of Jews were stranded in Europe, many of whom became victims of Hitler's Final Solution.[88]

In 1941, Haj al-Hussein, the Grand Mufti of Jerusalem, met with Hitler in Berlin to express solidarity with Hitler and the Nazi cause. He was also there to discuss what should be done to Germany's Jews.

Recently, Prime Minister Netanyahu claimed the "Final Solution" was in fact Husseini's idea.[89] His claim was strongly criticised, as it might be misconstrued to lessen Hitler's guilt. However, we cannot dispute that Husseini, representing the Arab population living in British mandated Palestine, met Hitler and enthusiastically supported his planned annihilation of European Jews.

## British Obstacles

Even after WWII ended and the horrors of the death camps became obvious, the British refused to allow all Jewish survivors to resettle in Palestine. At its peak in 1947, the Jewish displaced person population had reached approximately 250,000.[90] Despite a quarter of a million displaced Jews, Britain set a quota of just 18,000 Jews per year to migrate to Palestine. In the three years that followed, illegal immigration became the major method of Jewish immigration to Palestine. Sixty-six illegal boats were organised during those years, but only around 80,000 illegal immigrants arrived in Palestine.

One such migrant vessel, the *Exodus*, arrived in Palestine in 1947, carrying 4,500 immigrants, but it was immediately sent back to Europe by the mandatory government. The British stopped other vessels carrying immigrants and interned the people in Cyprus. Most of these Jews arrived in Israel only after the establishment of the state.

It would not be a bridge too far to conclude that despite the Balfour Declaration, San Remo, and other resolutions, Britain now opposed the idea of a Jewish homeland in Palestine. Despite Britain's commitment to a Jewish homeland in the years following WWI they abstained in the UN vote in 1947 that established the Jewish homeland.

## America Too Is Answerable

As earlier as 1942, the United States of America knew of Hitler's plan to annihilate the European Jews. A report smuggled from Poland to London described in detail the killing centres at Chelmno and the use of gas vans. It was estimated that at this stage, 700,000 people had already perished.[91]

What was the United States' response? Anti-Semitism, which saw the Jews blamed for the Great Depression,[92] caused the US to close its doors to fleeing Jews. In the years leading up to the end of the war, America received only 132,000 Jewish refugees, just 10 per cent of the quota allowed by their own laws.[93]

In 1939, Congress refused to raise immigration quotas to admit 20,000 Jewish children fleeing the Nazis. As if to add insult to injury, the wife of the US Commissioner of Immigration remarked at a cocktail party, "20,000 children would all too soon grow up to be 20,000 ugly adults."[94]

Finally, in January 1944, Secretary of the Treasury Henry Morgenthau, as the only Jew in the Cabinet, presented President Roosevelt with a report he commissioned, titled, "Report to the Secretary on the Acquiescence of this Government in the Murder of the Jews." His report starts with this damning line: "One of the greatest crimes in history, the slaughter of the Jewish people in Europe, is continuing unabated."[95]

Morgenthau's report then makes this startling allegation of gross negligence and inaction against his own government:

> This Government has for a long time maintained that its policy is to work out programs to serve those Jews of Europe who could be saved.
> I am convinced on the basis of the information which is available to me that certain officials

in our State Department, which is charged with carrying out this policy, have been guilty not only of gross procrastination and wilful failure to act, but even of wilful attempts to prevent action from being taken to rescue Jews from Hitler.

I fully recognize the graveness of this statement and I make it only after having most carefully weighed the shocking facts which have come to my attention during the last several months.

Unless remedial steps of a drastic nature are taken, and taken immediately, I am certain that no effective action will be taken by this government to prevent the complete extermination of the Jews in German controlled Europe, and that this Government will have to share for all time responsibility for this extermination.[96]

He then turned his attention to the US State Department:

The tragic history of the Government's handling of this matter reveals that certain State Department officials are guilty of the following:

1) They have not only failed to use the Governmental machinery at their disposal to rescue Jews from Hitler, but have even gone so far as to use this Government machinery to prevent the rescue of these Jews.

2) They have not only failed to cooperate with private organizations in the efforts of these organizations to work out individual programs of their own, but have taken steps designed to prevent these programs from being put into effect.

3) They not only have failed to facilitate the obtaining of information concerning Hitler's plans to exterminate the Jews of Europe but in their official capacity have gone so far as to surreptitiously attempt to stop the obtaining of information concerning the murder of the Jewish population of Europe.

4) They have tried to cover up their guilt by:

    a. concealment and misrepresentation;

    b. the giving of false and misleading explanations for their failures to act and their attempts to prevent action; and

    c. the issuance of false and misleading statements concerning the "action" which they have taken to date.[97]

Shamed into action, Roosevelt created the War Refugee Board, which in turn set up refugee camps in Italy, North Africa, and the United States. However, that proved to be "too little, too late."

## The Bones Are Rattling

Could the result have been different if Britain and the United States relaxed restrictions on Jewish migration in the years leading up to the end of WWII?

Could millions of Jews been saved had Britain (and France) not allowed Haj al-Husseini, the Mufti of Jerusalem, to travel to Berlin to meet Hitler and encourage him in his efforts to exterminate the Jews?

There are so many ifs and buts, and we may never know the full story. The one thing we do know is that what the devil and Hitler meant for evil, God turned around for good. Despite the holocaust, British opposition to Jewish immigration, and the inaction of the United States, the Jews have survived, and what we have seen is a modern-day exodus.

Just as Pharaoh sought to exterminate the Hebrews but saw only a return of the Jews to the Promised Land, so too did Hitler's efforts at genocide only serve as strong motivation for the Jews to return to their Promised Land. In the years since WWII, the population of Israel has grown from 550,000 to over 8,000,000, and it continues to grow.

This was a miracle, but even greater miracles are continuing to unfold before our very eyes.

# CHAPTER 7
## Zechariah—The (Not So) Lost Tribes of Israel

*It is a miracle of biblical and historic proportions, and we are witnessing the words of the Prophets come to life before our very eyes*

—Michael Freund

In the previous chapter, we spoke of the Jews returning in greatly increased numbers to their Promised Land. When God made His covenant with Abraham, it involved a land and the descendants of Isaac and Jacob.[98] Jacob had twelve sons, and the Jews are the descendants of one of two of those twelve tribes of Judah and Benjamin.

In this chapter, we will see that there are other descendants of Jacob who seem lost to history but were never forgotten by God. One of the great miracles of our time is that groups of people, entire villages and communities, have been found to have religious customs and practices that are Hebraic in origin. With the aid of modern scientific practices in the field of DNA mapping, people from around the world have been verified as descendants of Jacob, and many have returned to Israel.

### All the Bones

God never left Ezekiel to wonder about the meaning of the dead, dry bones scattered in the valley. They were the whole house of Israel.[99] Ezekiel's prophecy is delivered after the nation of Israel had been split and ten of the tribes seemed lost forever and Judah was exiled to Babylon.

In biblical times, the nation of Israel that left Egypt under the leadership of Moses consisted of twelve tribes. Each tribe received an allotment of land, with the exception the priestly tribe of Levi. Levi was dispersed throughout the other tribes, and Joseph received a double portion through his sons, Ephraim and Manasseh. The thirteen tribes between them were allotted twelve parcels of land that made up the "Promised Land" given to Israel.

Under the kingship of Saul, David, and Solomon, the twelve tribes were united, but soon after Solomon's death, and centuries before Ezekiel's vision of dry, dead bones coming together, Israel was bitterly divided along family lines.[100]

In the south were the two tribes of Judah and Benjamin, known as the "Kingdom of Judah," and to the north was the "Kingdom of Israel," consisting of the other ten tribes.[101]

Due to sin and rebellion, the Northern Kingdom was taken captive by the Assyrians in 723 BC. One hundred and forty years later, Judah was taken captive by the Babylonians. Among the great mysteries of the Bible is the fate of the Northern Kingdom, the so-called Lost Tribes of Israel. We know what happened to Judah. While the Jews were in captivity, Babylon fell to the Medo-Persian Empire. After seventy years of captivity and the collapse of the Babylonian empire, during the reign of Cyrus the King of Persia, Judah began returning to their own land and rebuilt Jerusalem and the Temple. They remained in their land until they were exiled again by the Romans in 135 CE. However, the northern tribes simply appear to have vanished.

Leading up to independence in 1948, a healthy debate took place over what to call the re-established Jewish homeland. Theodor Herzl, as far back as the 1890s, referred to the dream of a homeland as "The Jewish State."[102] That name was also favoured by Ben Gurion. As independence was declared, rather than call the new homeland "The Jewish State," Ben Gurion said, "I hereby declare the establishment of a Jewish state in Eretz Yisrael, to be known as *The State of Israel*."

Whether he understood the full significance of what he said, we cannot be certain. By naming the newly formed state *Israel* and not *The Jewish State*, he declared a state for all twelve of Jacob's descendants whom Ezekiel saw that day. This was a promise from God and confirmed by Isaiah and other prophets.[103]

Ezekiel saw not just Jews but the *whole house of Israel* returning to their land.[104] As I've already said, the problem is that no one is certain where the Hebrews from the northern kingdom ended up after being taken captive. Their rejection and exile is recorded in 2 Kings 17.

> And the Lord rejected all the descendants of Israel, afflicted them, and delivered them into the hand of plunderers, until He had cast them from His sight. For He tore Israel from the house of David, and they made Jeroboam the son of Nebat king. Then Jeroboam drove Israel from following the Lord, and made them commit a great sin. For the children of Israel walked in all the sins of Jeroboam which he did; they did not depart from them, until the Lord removed Israel out of His sight, as He had said by all His servants the prophets. So Israel was carried away from their own land to Assyria, as it is to this day. (2 Kings 17:20–23)

For two hundred years from the time they split from Judah until they were finally driven from the land, the Northern Kingdom had nineteen kings, and not one of them is described as a "good king." Every king's obituary was the same: "He did evil in the sight of the Lord, and walked in the way of his father [and in the way of his mother] and in the way of Jeroboam the son of Nebat who had made Israel sin."[105,106]

Exiled by Assyria in 723 BC, these ten tribes appear lost to history. This in contrast to Judah, who also had nineteen kings (and one queen) in its 320 years before its final exile by Babylon in 588 BC; they had eight godly kings, such as Josiah and Jehosophat. Because of God's promise to David that his kingdom would be everlasting, the Jews returned to their land in just seventy years to rebuild Jerusalem and the temple.[107]

So what did happen to the "lost tribes?"

Messianic Jew and Biblical scholar Dr Michael L Brown says that there are a few possible explanations as to what happened to these tribes:

> (1) Some of the people remained in Samaria and became known as the Samaritans.[108]
>
> (2) Some of the people may have made their way to Judah and became incorporated into the larger "Jewish" population (see especially 2 Chronicles 34:3-9, which indicates that a remnant of the ten northern tribes remained intact after the Assyrian exile). This is reflected in New Testament references that speak of "the twelve tribes of Israel" (see Acts 26:7; James 1:1)[109]
>
> (3) Some of the people became completely assimilated into the nations where they were scattered and have become lost to history.[110]
>
> (4) Some may have actually retained their Israelite-Jewish origins, retaining their ancient traditions and continuing to preserve a conscious identification as Israelites or Jews.[111]

The truth is that these ten tribes only appeared to be lost. They have never been lost to God because of His covenant with Abraham. The covenant, confirmed through Jacob, ensures that God is not just bringing Judah (the Jews) home ; He is also bringing Jacob's entire family home.

Consider Zechariah's prophecy, written centuries after Israel's exile:

> Those of Ephraim shall be like a mighty man,
> And their heart shall rejoice as if with wine.
> Yes, their children shall see it and be glad;
> Their heart shall rejoice in the Lord.
> I will whistle for them and gather them,
> For I will redeem them;
> And they shall increase as they once increased.
> I will sow them among the peoples,

> And they shall remember Me in far countries;
> They shall live, together with their children,
> And they shall return. (Zechariah 10:7–9)

The reference to Ephraim is a reference to the ten lost tribes of Israel.[112] The so called lost tribes will be like a mighty man and rejoice and be glad because God is calling them back home and promising that they will flourish in their homeland. Isaiah confirms this when he says,

> It shall come to pass in that day
> That the Lord shall set His hand again the second time
> To recover the remnant of His people who are left,
> From Assyria and Egypt,
> From Pathros and Cush,
> From Elam and Shinar,
> From Hamath and the islands of the sea. (Isaiah 11:11)

One of the signs that mark the end of the age is the return of the lost tribes of Israel to be united with Judah and the nation of Israel is reborn.

## Benjamin of Tudela

Benjamin of Tudela was a medieval traveller who journeyed through Europe and Asia. Between 1159 and 1172 he visited several Jewish and non-Jewish communities around the world, writing extensively of his experiences. His travel diary, *The Book of Travels*, has become a primary research source for medieval historians.

While in Persia, he wrote,

> There are men of Israel in the land of Persia who say that in the mountains dwell four of the tribes of Israel, namely, the tribe of Dan, the tribe of Zebulun, the tribe of Asher, and the tribe of Naphtali. They are governed by their own prince, Joseph the Levite. Among them are learned scholars. [113]

While on the Arabian Peninsula he came across a large Jewish settlement and recorded that these tribesmen were "of the tribes Reuben and Gad, and the half-tribe of Manasseh. Their seat of government is a great city surrounded by the mountains of the North. The Jews of Kheibar have built many large fortified cities."[114]

Benjamin has made claims that in the twelfth century, there were survivors who had traced their ancestry back to the Northern Kingdom and its seventh-century-BC exile. There has been debate as to the accuracy of his reports, but it is certain that his work has inspired many to seek out and find the ten "lost tribes."

Jewish Voice Ministries is dedicated reaching the lost tribes through medical clinics and humanitarian aid and spiritual outreach in Africa and India.[115] The International Christian Embassy in Jerusalem is also assisting several groups claiming to have links to the lost tribes return to the Promised Land.[116]

## DNA Testing Finds Lost Tribes—Tracing the Priesthood (Cohanim)

The Cohanim are direct male descendants of Aaron. For the three thousand years since Moses anointed his older brother, Aaron, as Israel's first high priest, the priesthood has been handed down from father to son to son. If the priesthood followed that tradition, then the Y chromosomes of the Levites today should bear some resemblance to one another because of their unbroken link back to Aaron.[117,118] Modern scientific practice has provided a breakthrough in the identification of the lost tribes through DNA testing of the Cohanim.[119]

Genetic studies among priests confirm that 50 per cent of Cohanim Jewish communities have an unusual set of genetic markers[120] on their Y chromosome. This chromosome is rarely found outside Jewish communities. There are communities throughout the world that for centuries were thought to have been lost who have this distinct genetic link to Aaron, Israel's first high priest.[121] This is the first miracle in the scientific identification of the lost tribes.

There are always minute changes occurring in DNA that build from generation to generation. By tracking these changes, scientists can estimate the number of generations back to a common ancestor. In the case of the Levites, that ancestor is Aaron. The second miracle is that the evidence suggests the priestly chromosomes come together at a date that roughly corresponds with the generation the Aaronic Priesthood is thought to have begun.[122]

## The Bene Israel

DNA testing is a powerful tool that is being used to track down the lost tribes. However, results have occasionally proven to be inconclusive. In other cases, they have been conclusive, as with the "Bene Israel."[123] The Bene Israel is a community in India, and DNA has confirmed a direct link to the Cohanim Y chromosome.

It is believed that Bene Israel reached India as long ago as 175 BC, when seven Jewish families were shipwrecked off the Konkan Coast, 100 km south of Mumbai, at Alibag. The shipwreck meant they lost all their religious books, leaving them only with the Shema, the Jewish prayer expressing one's faith in God.[124]

> Sh'ma Yisra'eil Adonai Eloheinu Adonai echad.
> (Hear, Israel, the Lord is our God, the Lord is One.)

The families grew and integrated with the local Indian population, adopting their language, dress, and food. The indigenous community called them the *śaniwar telī*, as they abstained from work on Saturdays, the Jewish Sabbath.[125] When this small community was found, they were observing the strict Jewish dietary laws, circumcision, and many of the Jewish festivals, in addition to their observance of the Sabbath. They did not celebrate Hanukkah, since that feast celebrates the second-century-BC victory of Jews over Greeks, long after the Bene Israel departed from the land of Israel.[126]

## Some of the Other "Not So" Lost Tribes of Israel

There are other groups all over the world, in Africa, Asia, the Americas, and Europe, that are believed to be descended from the lost tribes. For example, in James Adair's book, *The History of the Indians*, he presented twenty-three arguments that "prove" the North American Indians were descended from the Ten Lost Tribes.[127] Others claim the South American Incas have links to Israel. While some of this is pure conjecture, there are groups, tribes, and villages that have had no known contact with the Israelites yet have many similarities with Hebrew tradition and religious belief. Below are a few more examples:

1. The Bnei Menashe[128]

The Bnei Menashe, descendants from the tribe of Manasseh.
On October 11, 2012, in an opinion piece titled, "Homecoming for a Lost Tribe of Israel," Michael Freund said that these people are returning after nearly 2,700 years of exile:

> The return of the Bnei Menashe to Israel is an inspiring story of Jewish faith, survival and dedication, and it marks the closing of an historical circle after 27 centuries of exile.
>
> It is a miracle of biblical and historic proportions, and we are witnessing the words of the

Prophets come to life before our very eyes.[129]

The Bnei Menashe are returning to Israel aided by the International Christian Embassy Jerusalem, which in itself is a fulfilment of Isaiah 49:22:

> [Nations] shall bring your sons [Israel] in their arms
> And your daughters shall be carried on their shoulders.

2. The Lemba, The Black Jews of Southern Africa

A black African tribe called the Lemba claim to have Jewish ancestry. Tudor Parfitt, a British historian who specialises in the study of Jewish communities, went to southern Africa to study their traditions. He concluded that the origin of many of them was Middle Eastern and not African. Parfitt could not decide whether these traditions were Islamic or Jewish in origin. Parfitt used DNA testing and showed their ancestors were Hebrew. He wrote, "Members of the priestly clan of the Lemba, known as the Buba, were even discovered to have a genetic element also found among the Jewish priestly line."[130]

A member of Parfitt's team Dr. David Goldstein commented on the findings.[131]

> The first striking thing about the Y chromosomes of the Lemba is that you find this particular chromosomal type (Cohen modal haplotype) that is characteristic of the Jewish priesthood in a frequency that is similar to what you see in major Jewish populations. Something just under one out of every 10 Lemba that we looked at had this particular Y chromosomal type that appears to be a signature of Jewish ancestry. Perhaps even more striking is the fact that this Cohen genetic signature is strongly associated with a particular clan in the Lemba. Most of the Cohen modal haplotypes that we observe are carried by individuals of the Buba clan which, in Lemba oral tradition, had a leadership role in bringing the Lemba out of Israel."[132]

DNA testing of the Lemba tribe of Zimbabwe shows that another *lost* tribe is not lost at all.

3. Beta Israel

Beta Israel claims to be direct decadents from the *lost* tribe of Dan. They claim that to avoid a war between Judah and Israel, Dan moved to Egypt and from there followed the Nile into Ethiopia.[133] Beta Israel has a long history of practicing such Jewish traditions as *kashrut*, Sabbath, and Passover.[134] It was for this reason their Jewish ancestry was accepted by the Chief Rabbinate of Israel and the Israeli government in 1975.[135] Subsequently, they emigrated to Israel *en masse* during the 1980s and 1990s, as Jews, under the Law of Return, during Israel's Operation Moses and Operation Solomon.[136]

4. The Pashtuns

The Pashtuns are a group consisting of 15 million people from sixty tribes. The 15 million Pashtuns live in a region that straddles the boundaries between Afghanistan, Pakistan, and Kashmir.

The *Guardian* newspaper in the UK reported on the Pathans in January 2010.

> Israel is to fund a rare genetic study to determine whether there is a link between the lost tribes of Israel and the Pashtuns of Afghanistan and northern Pakistan.
>
> Historical and anecdotal evidence strongly suggests a connection, but definitive scientific proof has never been found. Some leading Israeli anthropologists believe that, of all the many groups in the world who claim a connection to the ten lost tribes, the Pashtuns, or Pathans, have the most compelling case.[137]

As we know that the Assyrians carried the ten tribes into captivity and most were dispersed in an area around modern-day northern Iraq and Afghanistan, the likelihood of the Pashtuns connection is very strong.

The Pashtuns have a proud oral history of direct decent from Israel, and their tribal names bear a striking resemblance to the ten tribes. These names include Yusufzai, which means "sons of Joseph," and Afridi, thought by some to come from Ephraim.

Although there are apparently strong traditional links to Israel, the *Guardian* went on to add,

> Paradoxically it is from the Pashtuns that the ultra-conservative Islamic Taliban movement in Afghanistan emerged. Pashtuns themselves sometimes talk of their Israelite connection, but show few signs of sympathy with, or any wish to migrate to, the modern Israeli state.[138]

5. Bene Ephraim

The Bene Ephraim, also called Telugu Jews because they speak Telugu, are a small community of Jews living primarily in Kottareddipalem, a village outside Guntur, India.[139] While their claim to be descended from Ephraim is disputed, there is no doubt that there exist strong links to Israel.

Certain oral traditions among Bene Ephraim, known as Cavilah traditions, have many customs and habits with Hebraic roots.[140] These include eating kosher meat, marriage under *chuppah*, burial customs, seven-day purification, and bar mitzvah.[141,142]

6. Ebos

On Sept 6, 2006, Israel recognised that the Ebos on the west coast of Africa in Nigeria as descendents from the tribes of Gad, Zebulun, and Issachar, from Ephraim.

7. Asia

In addition to several tribes and villages with strong ties to the Hebrews, in both Korea and Japan there are many names and places that are very Hebrew sounding. This has led many to believe that the ten lost tribes found their way to the Far East. It is yet to see whether DNA testing will prove or disprove Israelite heritage.

## Conclusion

Judah was exiled to Babylon while the Northern Kingdom was dispersed throughout the world. For centuries, they seemed lost. The Northern Kingdom, however, was never lost to God. He knows exactly where they are, and He is bringing them all home again. He is doing this in fulfilment of many prophecies.

> But I will gather the remnant of My flock out of all countries where I have driven them, and bring them back to their folds; and they shall be fruitful and increase. (Jeremiah 23:3)

DNA testing is proving invaluable in determining the Hebraic roots of many groups and villages with priestly links to Aaron. And as the bones of the *whole house of Israel* are rattling, so to the devil is trying to rattle the world in his futile attempts to thwart God's plan and purpose for His people.

# CHAPTER 8
## Joel—Israel, an Undivided Nation

*Our right to this land, in its entirety, is enduring and eternal. And until the coming of the Redemption, we shall never yield this historic right.*

—David Ben-Gurion,
Speech to the Twenty-first Zionist Congress

In the previous chapters, we studied three modern-day miracles. In chapter 5, we studied the miracle of the rebirth of a nation. Israel was born in a day, fulfilling Isaiah's prophecy. In chapter 6, we examined the influx of Jews to their promised land. In the previous chapter, we saw that after millennia of exile, the *lost tribes* from the Northern Kingdom are returning to Israel. Multiple prophecies predicted the return of the *whole house of Israel* to the Promised Land and we are seeing these fulfilled before our very eyes.

One would think the world would stop and consider these three momentous events and give God the glory. The reality is that the Arab world, in partnership with the United Nations, continues to attack Israel and her right to exist. Nation after nation urges Israel to surrender land in exchange for peace. God foresaw all this and spoke through the ancient prophets making it clear that He will never allow His land to be divided. We will also see that the Arabs that cry the loudest for a divided Israel don't want a divided land, rather they seek the expulsion of all Jews from the land. Finally, the nations that desire to divide Israel to appease the Arabs will be judged harshly by God.

### A Warning—Don't Touch the Apple of God's Eye

There is coming a day when God will judge the nations of the world based on their treatment of the "apple of His eye."[143] To understand why this will happen, we need to contrast two covenants we have already discussed in chapter 2.

The Mosaic Covenant is a conditional and a temporal covenant that God made with Moses on behalf of Israel while in the Sinai. It is temporal because it is replaced by a *New Covenant* that the prophets promised.[144] It is conditional because if Israel obeyed God, she would be blessed, but failure to obey would mean curses.[145] The final curse would be exile, and the nation would be scattered throughout the world, where they would suffer anguish and turmoil.[146] However, there is another covenant that God made. This one was with Abraham and was sealed in blood. Zechariah says that it is because of the blood of the covenant that God will set Israel free from bondage.[147] It is unconditional and was never based Israel's faithfulness solely on God's commitment to His promise.[148] God warned Israel that failure to keep the Mosaic Covenant would end in exile, but because of the Abrahamic Covenant, He would bring them home, and the nations that mistreated the exiled Jews would be judge appropriately. The nations would also be judged by how they treated the land. Joel says,

> I will also gather all nations,
> And bring them down to the Valley of Jehoshaphat;
> And I will enter into judgment with them there
> On account of My people, My heritage Israel,
> Whom they have scattered among the nations;
> THEY HAVE ALSO DIVIDED UP MY LAND. (Joel 3:2)

Joel made the point 2,500 years ago that God would judge the nations on account of His people and because they seek to divide the land. God calls it *My* land; it is neither Israel's nor the Arab's. Israel, the Arabs, and the United Nations do not have the right to negotiate to give "land for peace," a notion not lost on Ben Gurion in 1937.

> No Jew is at liberty to surrender the right of the Jewish Nation and the Land of Israel to exist. No Jewish body is sanctioned to do so. Even all the Jews alive today have no authority to yield any piece of land whatsoever. This right is reserved to the Jewish People throughout the generations. This right cannot be forfeited under any circumstances. Even if at some given time there will be those who declare that they are relinquishing this right, they have neither the power nor the authority to negate it for future generations. The Jewish Nation is neither obligated by nor responsible for any such waiver. Our right to this land, in its entirety, is enduring and eternal. And until the coming of the Redemption, we shall never yield this historic right.[149]

Dividing the land will never succeed, because God doesn't approve. As Israeli Prime Minister Benjamin Netanyahu declared, "Israel could never, ever countenance a fully sovereign Palestinian state."

Both Ben Gurion and Netanyahu's statements address the issue of dividing the land west of the Jordan, modern-day Israel. The problem, however, existed long before Ben Gurion spoke in 1937. As we discovered in chapter 5, the idea of dividing the land goes as far back as 1921, when Churchill sought to redefine the term "in Palestine." This led to the idea of *Jewish Palestine* and *Arab Transjordan*, and the seeds for dividing the land were sown.

## United Nations Resolution 181

As we have already discussed, on November 29, 1947, the United Nations voted to partition Palestine into Jewish and Palestinian states. The vote further divided God's land and left Jerusalem as an "international city," to be governed by the UN, because it acknowledged the religious significance of the city to the Jews, Christians, and Muslims.[150]

Israel reluctantly accepted the UN resolution, and in May 1948, Israel was declared a nation, based on UN Resolution 181. The Arabs, however, chose war.

## The War of Independence 1948-49

The day after Israel's independence, the Arab nations invaded with the stated aim of annihilating Israel. The war lasted over twelve months, and when the armistice was declared, there were four significant changes to the proposed borders.

Israel's 1947 borders gave them three parcels of land that were not joined, but after the war, the land called Israel was all unified.[151]

Secondly, according the "Mandate of Palestine," 77 per cent of Israel was under Israeli jurisdiction, a significant increase.

Thirdly, there were no Palestinians. The Gaza Strip was considered part of Egypt, and the Arabs in Gaza called themselves Egyptians. The West Bank and East Jerusalem formed the western region of Jordan, and Arabs there called themselves Jordanians. It would be another eighteen years before the Arabs in Israel called themselves Palestinians.[152]

Finally, Jerusalem was not the international city the UN planned but was divided: West Jerusalem, the "New City," was in Israel, and East Jerusalem, the "Old City," was in Jordan.

## The Six-Day War

The next major conflict was the Six-Day War, fought in June 1967 and was instigated by the Egyptians. On May 16, Egypt ordered all the United Nations Forces stationed on the Egyptian-Israeli border to withdraw. This act removed the international buffer that had existed between Egypt and Israel since the Suez Crisis.[153]

Six days later, they announced a blockade of all goods to and from Israel, which international law deems to be an act of war. Israel responded with a preemptive strike. Within hours the largest and most modern Arab air force was decimated. Egypt lied to her allies and claimed to have won significant victories, which gave Jordan and Syria a false hope and led to Jordanian attacks from the West Bank and Syrian air strikes from the north. After just six days, the Arabs sued for peace, having suffered a humiliating defeat, losing control of Gaza, the West Bank, Golan Heights and Sinai Peninsula to the Israelis.[154] Israel was now undivided and in possession of a large section of the land promised to Abraham by God.

The greatest victory of all was that the old city of Jerusalem and the temple mount were in Jewish hands for the first time since 135 AD. This was a cause for great rejoicing in Israel: even though it did not reflect the British commitment in the Balfour Declaration, it did reflect Churchill's white paper, and Israel's "eternal city" had been liberated.

Despite lasting just six days, the ramifications of this war are still being felt and hotly debated fifty years later. The defeat gave rise to the "Palestinian psyche." Arabs living in Gaza would no longer call themselves Egyptian, and those living in the West Bank would no longer call themselves Jordanians; rather, they all began referring to themselves Palestinians and invented their own ongoing connection to the land, demanding that Israel again be a divided land.

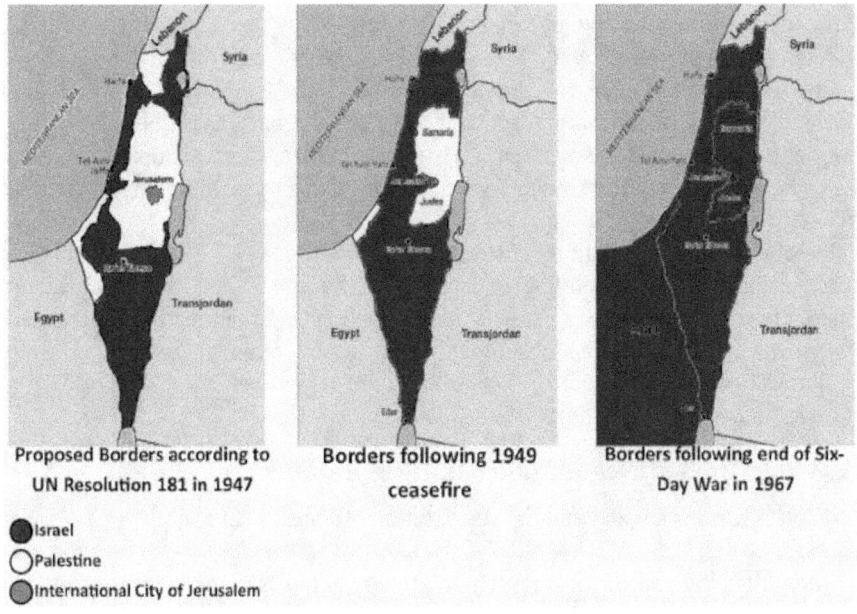

| Figure 3 - | Figure 4 - | Figure 5 - |
| Borders determined by UN Resolution 181 | 1949 Armistice Lines | Israel after 1967 war |

## The Yom Kippur War (1973)

The Six-Day War was followed by years of intermittent skirmishes that culminated in a full-scale war in 1973. On the afternoon of October 6, during the Jewish Festival of Yom Kippur, Israel was invaded as the Egyptians crossed the Suez Canal to attack from the south, while Syrian forces attempted to take the Golan Heights in the north.

Within a few days, the Israel Defence Forces had turned things around. Having struck the Egyptian air defences, Israel crossed the Suez Canal and surrounded the Egyptian Third Army. In the Golan Heights, Israel suffered many casualties but managed to force the Syrians to retreat, and they advanced to the edge of the Golan plateau on the road to Damascus. This war threatened to bring Russia and the United States directly into the conflict.

On October 22, the United Nations Security Council adopted Resolution 338, which called for an immediate end to the fighting; fighting continued for several days and finally ended on October 25.

As in all the preceding wars, Yom Kippur had far-reaching implications.

Following the ceasefire, Israel gained territory in the Golan Heights, bordering Syria. Israel still occupies that territory as a buffer against Syria because of her constant threats and alliance with Hezbollah. Israel also occupied land on Egyptian side of the Suez Canal. As we will see six years later, they returned that occupied land to Egypt.

Despite all the protestations of the Arabs, this was never a battle about justice for the oppressed Arabs living in Israel. For the aggressors, it was all about jihad, the sole intention was Israel's annihilation. The Israeli leadership realised there was no guarantee she would always be so dominant against an Arab military apparatus hell bent on her destruction. Israel has set about building a military that would stand against all Arab assaults.

## A Whole Host of Negotiations and Resolutions

1. UN Resolution 242 and the Recognition of Palestinian Rights

Soon after the end of the Six-Day War, the United Nations Security Council unanimously passed Resolution 242 and demanded Israel withdraw from the territories it now occupied to the pre-war borders. That position has never changed. The question we will never know the answer to is what would the UN say if the Arabs occupied land held by Israel before the Six-Day War? Would there have been Resolution 242 demanding Arab withdrawal? Probably not. We do know for certain that if there had been such a resolution, the Arabs would contravene it, because their stated aim has always been the annihilation of Israel.

2. The EU Foreign Affairs Council

Following Yom Kippur, on November 6, 1973, just two weeks after the cessation of hostilities, the European Union's Foreign Affairs Council met and discussed the ongoing hostilities in the Middle East. In their resolution, they said any peace agreement should be based on mutual respect and both Jew and Arab had the right to live securely and at peace within recognised boundaries. However, when they defined those boundaries, they made two contradictory statements.

Firstly, EU foreign ministers coined the phrase, "the inadmissibility of the acquisition of territory by force," saying any land acquired because of war did not form the basis of new borders. On the surface, that is a fair starting point.

The problem is that they went on to state that Israel's borders were to be the pre-1967 borders, borders that were determined by the War of Independence. The only consistent position must be borders based on the UN Resolution 181. Something Arabs have constantly opposed because of Jerusalem.

3. PLO Acceptance of Two-State Solution

In the mid-1970s, the PLO for the first time acknowledged it was willing to accept Israel's right to exist.[155] That acknowledgement came with the rider *in the interim*. The PLO was telling the world, "Yes, we will accept a divided Israel as an interim measure, as we move towards a united *Arab Palestine*."

This attitude is born out in a 2011 poll by Stanley Greenberg and the Palestinian Centre for Public Opinion.[156] Sponsored by the Israel Project, the results revealed that 61 per cent of Palestinians rejected a two-state solution, while 34 per cent said they accepted it.[157] Of the respondents, *66 per cent said the Palestinians' real goal should be to start with a two-state solution but then proceed to forming a single Palestinian state.*[158]

4. The Egypt-Israel Peace Treaty

The Egypt-Israel Peace Treaty, which was signed by Egyptian President Anwar Sadat, US President Jimmy Carter, and Israeli Prime Minister Menachem Begin, at the White House on March 26, 1979, saw Israel return the Sinai Peninsula to Egypt.

The deal was not a great treaty for Israel but did reveal to the world that Israel was willing to negotiate and even give up land for peace, if its security could be assured.

The problem has always been that Arabs have refused to guarantee that Israel would be left to live at peace within agreed borders. Despite that, several meetings have been held that have resulted in Israel's withdrawal, at great risk to her safety, from the West Bank and Gaza.

5. Oslo (1993)

A series of secret meetings were held between Israeli and Palestinian negotiators, hosted by Norway. These meetings produced the 1993 Oslo Peace Accord and led to the transfer some of powers and responsibilities in the Gaza

Strip and West Bank from Israel to the Palestinians in the mid-1990s.[159]

6. 1996–99

In 1996, then–prime minister Benjamin Netanyahu, clearly frustrated by the PLO's leadership reticence (or inability) to stop suicide attacks by Hamas and Palestinian Islamic jihad, adopted a policy he called "reciprocity," whereby Israel would no longer engage in the peace process if the PLO continued the incitement and support of terrorism.

This continues to be his position, which is totally understandable.

7. Camp David 2000 Summit

With the peace process stalled and a new prime minister in Israel, US President Bill Clinton met with Yasser Arafat and Israeli Prime Minister Ehud Barak.

At that time, Israel offered to "return" to the Palestinians up to 66 per cent of the "occupied land" and pay compensation to the Palestinians who lost land. Arafat rejected this offer outright and never sought to put forward a counter-offer. The Palestinian position has always remained intractable.

Journalist and author, Nathan Thrall, shows this to be case in his book *What Future for Israel?*

> At his Jerusalem residence on September 16, 2008, Israeli Prime Minister Ehud Olmert showed Palestinian President Mahmoud Abbas a map representing the most far-reaching territorial compromise ever proposed by an Israeli premier. According to Olmert, his plan granted the Palestinians a state with a land area equal to 99.5 percent of the West Bank and Gaza. Israel would annex 6.3 percent of Palestinian territory, compensating the Palestinians with Israeli lands equivalent to 5.8 percent, as well as a corridor that would connect the two regions but remain under Israeli sovereignty. Jerusalem would be a shared capital, its eastern, Arab neighbourhoods part of Palestine, its Jewish neighbourhoods in both halves of the city part of Israel, and a roughly two-square-kilometre area encompassing Jerusalem's Old City would be under international administration.
>
> Olmert has said to numerous interviewers that he told Abbas it was the best offer any Israeli leader would give in the next fifty years. Abbas asked to take the map to show to his experts. Olmert refused, fearing that Abbas would pocket it and insist that it serve as a new starting point for future talks. The two agreed that their negotiators would meet the following day. In the years that followed, Olmert frequently asserted that he never heard from Abbas again. "I've been waiting," he recently said, "ever since."[160]

## A Two-State Non-Solution

It is a myth to say that Israel is intransigent, refusing to negotiate, while the Arabs are flexible and wanting to negotiate. The evidence proves the opposite. Since 1973, the UN and world powers have been looking for ways to divide Israel against God's will, and contrary to the intent of the post–World War I resolutions, Israel for seventy years has been the one willing to negotiate and even surrender land to find a solution.

On the other hand, Hamas said that it would never accept the two-state solution or give up one inch of the land of Palestine while reiterating its call to the Palestinian Authority president, Mahmoud Abbas, to immediately halt the negotiations with Israel, declaring "resistance in all shapes, first and foremost armed struggle will remain the only effective way to achieve the goals of the Palestinian people and liberate their land."[161]

Its announcement came in response to statements attributed to Abbas to the effect that the Islamist movement had "authorised" him to agree to the establishment of a Palestinian state along the pre-1967 lines.

Hamas said it never gave Abbas or anyone else a mandate to agree to the two-state solution.

Their charter clearly states that the aim of Arabs is a "one-state" solution, a Palestinian state; they see themselves as "one of the links in the chain of the struggle against the Zionist invaders," believing that Palestine is Islamic land. They do not want a peaceful solution and declare that the armed struggle will continue.

> Article 13: (Peaceful Solutions, Initiatives and International Conferences) Initiatives, and so-called peaceful solutions and international conferences, are in contradiction to the principles of the Islamic Resistance Movement ... These conferences are only ways of setting the infidels in the land of the Moslems as arbitrators. When did the infidels do justice to the believers? ... There is no solution for the Palestinian question except through Jihad.[162]

> Article 15: (The Jihad for the Liberation of Palestine is an Individual Duty) The day that enemies usurp part of Moslem land, Jihad becomes the individual duty of every Moslem. In face of the Jews' usurpation of Palestine, it is compulsory that the banner of Jihad be raised.[163]

Their charter makes this battle over Israel an eschatological battle:

> The Day of Judgement will not come about until Moslems fight the Jews (killing the Jews), when the Jew will hide behind stones and trees. The stones and trees will say O Moslems, O Abdulla, there is a Jew behind me, come and kill him. Only the Gharkad tree, (evidently a

certain kind of tree) would not do that because it is one of the trees of the Jews.[164]

I believe Mike Huckabee, former Arkansas governor, got it right when he said in a speech on December 3, 2015, at the Republican Jewish Coalition Presidential Forum,

> I consider [the two-state solution] no solution whatsoever. There cannot be two states [trying to own] the same piece of real estate especially when one of those states does not believe the other one even has a right to exist much less exist peacefully.
>
> You can't have two governments wanting to own the same piece of real estate, so why don't we leave it in the hands of the government to whom it was originally given and why don't we leave it into the hands of those who will protect not only the antiquities but respect the religions, not only of the Jews, but also of the Muslims, and of the Christians.[165]

While Hamas makes no secret of the fact that their goal is the destruction of Israel, two-thirds of all Palestinians believe a two-state solution is only as a foundation for a one-state Palestine. The rest of the world, from the UN to the EU and even to the White House, diplomats, presidents, and foreign ministers still posit that a two-state solution is the only solution. Former US President Barack Obama, while still in office, stated,

> We reiterate the urgent need for a two-state solution between Israelis and Palestinians ... I continue to believe that a two-state solution is absolutely vital for not only peace between Israelis and Palestinians, but for the long-term.[166]

Thomas Friedman, the 1983 and 1988 Pulitzer Prize winner for international reporting, has been criticised by supporters of both sides of the Arab-Israeli conflict, which shows me that his views are measured, and when he says that the two-state solution is dead, we should at least take notice.

> The peace process is dead. It's over ... The next U.S. president will have to deal with an Israel determined to permanently occupy all the territory between the Jordan River and the Mediterranean Sea, including where 2.5 million West Bank Palestinians live.
>
> How did we get there? So many people stuck knives into the peace process it's hard to know who delivered the mortal blow. Was it the fanatical Jewish settlers determined to keep expanding their footprint in the West Bank and able to sabotage any Israeli politician or army officer who opposed them? Was it right-wing Jewish billionaires, like Sheldon Adelson, who used their influence to blunt any U.S. congressional criticism of Bibi Netanyahu?
> Or was it Netanyahu, whose lust to hold onto his seat of power is only surpassed by his lack

of imagination to find a secure way to separate from the Palestinians? Bibi won: He's now a historic figure—the founding father of the one-state solution.[167]

This is a rather pointed rebuke of the Israeli side of this process, particularly for Netanyahu, who he called "the founding father of a 'one-state solution'," but if the Israeli prime minister was the founding father, who is the mother? He then turned his attention to the Palestinians and gave the answer to this question:

> Hamas is the mother. Hamas devoted all its resources to digging tunnels to attack Israelis from Gaza rather than turning Gaza into Singapore, making a laughingstock of Israeli peace advocates. And Hamas launched a rocket close enough to Tel Aviv's airport that the U.S. banned all American flights for a day, signalling to every Israeli, dove or hawk, what could happen if they ceded the West Bank.
>
> But Hamas was not alone. The Palestinian president, Mahmoud Abbas, sacked the only effective Palestinian Prime Minister ever, Salam Fayyad, who was dedicated to fighting corruption and proving that Palestinians deserved a state by focusing on building institutions, not U.N. resolutions.
>
> They all killed the two-state solution. Let the one-state era begin. It will involve a steady low-grade civil war between Palestinians and Israelis and a growing Israeli isolation in Europe and on college campuses that the next U.S. president will have to navigate.[168]

The reality is that since 1993, nearly two and a half decades of peace negotiations between the Israelis and the Palestinians, failure has always been the outcome. Some blame Israel, others the Palestinians, while others say it is the Israeli settlers or Palestinian terrorists responsible for failed outcomes. Still others, like Friedman, single out the leadership.

The reality is if the foundation is flawed, nothing can stand. The reason for the failed process lies squarely with the Palestinians' refusal to recognise the state of Israel. At the heart of the Oslo Accords was a belief that both the Israelis and the Palestinians finally recognised the legitimacy of each other's national rights and aspirations.

With that foundation laid, all that remained was to work through complex but solvable issues of Jerusalem, the return of Palestinian refugees from 1948-9, and the burgeoning Israeli settlements in the West Bank. Yet despite the handshakes in Oslo, the Palestinians have steadfastly refused to acknowledge Israel's right to exist.

When Netanyahu made that the precursor to the resumption of talks, Abbas refused, saying, "Palestinians would never recognise the *Jewishness of the State of Israel.*"

The Gatestone Institute had this to say about this very issue:

> The core of the problem is that Palestinian recognition of Israel as the state of the Jewish People would not only end the dream of the return to Palestine, but also of the destruction of Israel currently being implemented through the incitement and terrorist campaign waged by the Palestinian People in their institutions, mosques, schools, terrorist organizations and foreign propaganda centres. Their strategic intention is to perpetuate the conflict, not end it.[169]

> The real reason Mahmoud Abbas wants control of the bridges and crossings, and refuses to leave them in Israeli hands, is to duplicate the terrorism of the Gaza Strip—to smuggle in arms and establish terrorist squads. Crossings left in Israel's hands would mean greater security for Jordan as well.[170]

What Gatestone is saying is what many have believed for years, that Palestinians do not want peace; they want Israel's destruction.

## God's Plan

The church has not replaced Israel as God's chosen people. He has never abandoned His covenant with Abraham, and He has a plan for His people, a plan that guarantees them a future, hope, and peace.[171] This plan cannot be separated from both the Land of Israel and her capital city, Jerusalem.

God makes a very specific promise in regard Israel's future, hope, and peace, promising to

> bring [Israel] out from the peoples and gather them from the countries, and I will bring them to their own land; I will feed them on the mountains of Israel, in the valleys and in all the inhabited places of the country. I will feed them in good pasture, and their fold shall be on the high mountains of Israel. (Ezekiel 34:13–14)

God's judgement is on the nations who seek to deny Israel's right to exist in their land.

> "You, son of man, prophesy to the mountains of Israel and say: 'Mountains of Israel, hear the word of Adonai. Thus says Adonai Elohim: "The enemy has said against you, 'Aha! Even the ancient high places have become our possession!' Therefore prophesy and say, thus says Adonai Elohim: 'Because they ravaged and crushed you from every side, so that you became the possession of the rest of the nations and you became the talk and evil gossip of people,' therefore, mountains of Israel, hear the word of Adonai, thus says Adonai Elohim to the mountains, the hills, the streams and the valleys, the desolate wastes and the cities that are forsaken, which have become prey and derision to the rest of the surrounding nations. Therefore, thus says Adonai Elohim: 'Surely in the fire of My wrath I have spoken against the

rest of the nations, and against all Edom, that have taken My land for themselves as a possession with the joy of all their heart and contempt in their souls, in order to seize it as plunder." (Ezekiel 36:1–5) [172]

## The Mountains of Israel

Thousands of years ago, Ezekiel declared there would come a day when the Jews would return to the land of Israel and when they did return they would resettle the mountains of Israel.

So where are the mountains of Israel?

This prophetic declaration is at the heart of the "problem"; what God calls "the mountains of Israel," the world calls the West Bank.

God's plan has always been to bring the Israelis home to an undivided land. He is bringing His people out from the nations He exiled them to and as they return they are going to occupy the mountains of the West Bank. It is here on the West Bank of the Jordan that the Israelis have the greatest connection to the land.

## The Ancient High Places

Ezekiel spoke of the Mountains of Israel but he also specifically mentioned the *ancient high places*. Abraham built four altars[173] during his lifetime in Shecham, Bethel, Hebron, and on Mount Moriah where he offered Isaac as a sacrifice.[174,175,176,177] All those locations have great historical and religious significance for the Jew; they prove Israel's ongoing connection to the land, and they are all located in the West Bank.

It was in Shecham that Abraham first settled when he entered the Promised Land. He bought a plot of land there, and Sarah is buried in the region.[178] Years later, Jacob brought more land in Shecham,[179] and it was in that plot of ground centuries later where Joshua buried Joseph's bones after the exodus.[180] The Biblical town of Shecham today is called Nablus, and is at the centre of the disputed West Bank. In just six months, from September 2015 to March 2016, there were eleven terrorist attacks in and around Nablus.

Abraham travelled around 30 km south, until he reached Bethel, where he built his second altar. It was here, in Bethel, where Jacob dreamed of a ladder ascending and descending to heaven.[181] Located on the Biblical site of Bethel is Beit El, an Israeli settlement and local council located in the West Bank. On October 23, 2015, an Israeli couple and their three young children were wounded when their car was firebombed by terrorists, and on January 31, 2016, three soldiers were shot at the nearby checkpoint.

Abraham's third altar was built in Hebron. Caleb received Hebron and the surrounding territory for his family after defeating the Anakim.[182] Later it served as a Levitical city and a city of refuge. It was in Hebron that David was anointed king of Judah, and he reigned over Israel from Hebron for seven and a half years before moving the capital to Jerusalem.[183]

Hebron, located just 30 km south of Jerusalem, is the second largest city in the West Bank, with a population of 200,000 Arabs and 1,000 Israeli settlers. The Oslo Accords divided Hebron into two sections: H1, which covers 80 per cent of the city and is under control of the Palestinian Authority, and H2, which is completely under Israeli military control. Approximately 160,000 Palestinians live in H1, while 40,000 Palestinians and 1,000 Israeli settlers live in H2.[184]

Hebron is also the centre of the ongoing sixty-year conflict between Israel and Palestine, and in just six months, from September 2015 to March 2016, there were no fewer than thirty-two terror attacks in Hebron or the surrounding areas, as well as at least four attacks elsewhere, carried out by terrorists from Hebron. Such is the turmoil in Hebron that the Australian Government issued this travel warning on January 17, 2017:

> There has been an increase in violent incidents in and around the Hebron area. Australians travelling to Hebron should keep up to date with local media reports and remain vigilant at all times.[185]

Abraham built one final altar, the most famous of all, when Abraham, with his son, Isaac, travelled to Mount Moriah. It was there that he built an altar and offered Isaac as a sacrifice to God. Before he could kill his son, God stepped in and provided a lamb.[186] David purchased the site where Abraham built his altar, and Solomon built the first temple over Abraham's altar. The Temple Mount is in East Jerusalem, and although Israel is now in possession of the "Old City" of Jerusalem, Israel's eternal city, it is still considered part of the West Bank and is the often referred to as the *most disputed real estate on the planet.*

Four *high places* all in the West Bank, the epitome of a divided Israel.

When nations recognise Israel's "ongoing connection" to the land and yet seek to partition the West Bank they forget it is in this region that Israel has the greatest connection.

## *Why Single Out Edom?*

God said He is angry with the nations because of their desire to divide Israel.

One nation comes in for special mention: Edom. Who is Edom and why does God single them out?

On May 25, 1946, the nation Ezekiel calls Edom, became known as the *Hashemite Kingdom of Transjordan*, commonly referred to as Jordan. But why is God singling them out above all the other nations? The War of Independence, which ended in March 1949, was for the Arab League a strategic failure, a defeat for Egypt and Arab-Palestine, a partial victory for Jordan, and a victory for Israel. What followed was a series of armistice agreements signed between Israel and the warring nations.

With Egypt, Lebanon, and Syria all sides withdrew to the borders of Mandatory Palestine, except for the Gaza Strip, which remained under Egyptian control. The last armistice agreement signed was with Jordan on April 3, 1949, who refused to withdraw to the pre-existent borders; instead, they kept control of all the areas they occupied, the West Bank and East Jerusalem.

Ezekiel's words—"A-ha! Even the ancient high places have become our possession"—were proving true with Jordan. Jordan was now in possession of the Mountains of Israel and her ancient high places. The fulfilment of this occurred on April 24, 1950, when Jordan formally annexed the West Bank and East Jerusalem and then thumbed its nose at the world and the Arab State in Palestine by changing its name to the Hashemite Kingdom of Jordan.[187]

Even since the liberation of Jerusalem, the Jordanian *waqf* have had full control of the temple mount.[188]

## Conclusion

People sympathetic to the Arab cause are quick to blame the Jews for the impasse in peace talks. Likewise, those who side with God's people, the Jews, blame the Arabs. The reality is that blame serves no useful purpose, but what is for certain is that God is using the current impasse to fulfil His plan of a united Israel, with Jerusalem as its capital.

# SECTION 3

# TENDONS, FLESH, AND SKIN (ISRAEL'S DEVELOPMENT)

# CHAPTER 9
## Ezekiel—Tendons (Israel's Resilience)

*If I had not fallen,*
*I would not have arisen.*
*Had I not been subject to darkness,*
*I could have not seen the light.*

—Midrash

In the previous sections, we saw how hatred of the Jews is a demonic response to God calling Israel to be His special people. Thousands of years of hostility and hatred from all over the world and violent jihad from all her Arab neighbours became the driving force behind the Zionist movement, which birthed the dream of millions of Jews to return to their land and build a Jewish state. Ezekiel's vision is being fulfilled before our very eyes. The vision saw dry dead bones coming together, not just Jewish bones but the bones of *the whole house of Israel*. Despite worldwide opposition and protests, Jews are returning to their own land after almost two thousand years in exile.

The vision doesn't end with dry, dead bones joining together.

> I will attach tendons to you and make flesh come upon you and cover you with skin; I will put breath in you, and you will come to life. Then you will know that I am the Lord ... I looked, and tendons and flesh appeared on them and skin covered them, but there was no breath in them. (Ezekiel 37:6, 8 New International Version)

Ezekiel sees tendons joining the bones together. Then muscle, a sign of power, attached to the bones. In the next chapter, we will look at Israel's growth to a powerhouse. After the muscle, skin covers the flesh, which gives beauty to the land. In chapter 11, we will see the transformation of the wasteland that was Palestine into the glorious land of Israel, fulfilling more Old Testament prophecies regarding Israel's return from exile.

### Israel, One Culture from Many Cultures

God promised that when the bones come together, tendons would appear on the bones. Biologically, tendons serve two purposes. Firstly, they join one bone to another. Since the late 1800s, Jews have returned to Israel from all points of the compass and diverse cultures to form one nation with one culture. Ayaan Hirsi Ali, in the *Jerusalem Post* on August 3, 2006, made this observation regarding the coming together of the nation of Israel.[189]

> I visited Israel a few years ago, primarily to understand how it dealt so well with so many immigrants from different origins ... I understood that a crucial element of success is the unifying factor among immigrants to Israel. Whether one arrives from Ethiopia or Russia, or one's grandparents emigrated from Europe, what binds them is being Jewish.[190]

She says that the secret of the coming together of Jews from all over the world and from diverse cultures is that they embrace the culture of Israel and do not hold onto their previous culture. She added that the immigrants to the Netherlands tend to hold to their old culture, which is problematic. Immigrants to Israel are Jewish, and it is their Jewishness that binds the bones together.

## Israel, a Most Resilient Nation

The second characteristic of tendons is their capacity to recover quickly and to spring back into shape. Tendons are resilient. If there is one word that describes the Jewish people, it would be resilient. No other nation has endured as much as Israel only to bounce back stronger each time. The Jewish people truly are resilient. The thousands of years of atrocities that culminated in the Nazi death camps and institutionalised racism would have destroyed any other nation, but not Israel. She has not only survived but has thrived. This was seen way back when Moses led the Hebrews out of Egypt.[191]

On January 16, 1996, then president of Israel, Ezer Weizmann, gave a speech to both houses of the German parliament to mark fifty years from the liberation from the death camps. He said,

> The very survival of the Jewish people through recorded time is nothing short of miraculous. The very fact that Jews exist as a nation today stands in testimony to the existence of God who acts in history. By any historical measure, the Jewish people should have disappeared long ago. The person who summed this up best was David Ben Gurion, the first Prime Minister of the State of Israel. He said: "A Jew who does not believe in miracles is not a realist." Why did he say that? Because miracles are the only possible explanation for the existence of the Jewish people.[192]

A survey of more than a billion people worldwide in 2014 was conducted by the Anti-Defamation League and found that 26 per cent harbour anti-Semitic views and 54 per cent, more than half the world's population, haven't heard of the holocaust.[193,194] Despite this, and the Arab nations stated aim to wipe out the Jews, Israel continues to prosper.

The following quotes from well-known people show the Jewish resilience:

> The Egyptian, the Babylonian, and the Persian rose, filled the planet with sound and splendour, then faded to dream-stuff and passed away; the Greek and the Roman followed; and made a vast noise, and they are gone; other people have sprung up and held their torch high for a time, but it burned out, and they sit in twilight now, or have vanished. The Jew saw them all, beat them all, and is now what he always was, exhibiting no decadence, no infirmities of age, no weakening of his parts, no slowing of his energies, no dulling of his alert and aggressive mind. All things are mortal but the Jew; all other forces pass, but he remains. What is the secret of his immortality?"
>
> —Mark Twain[195]

> Israel was not created to disappear - Israel will endure and flourish.
>
> —John F. Kennedy[196]

> What is the Jew? What kind of unique creature is this whom all the rulers of all the nations of the world have disgraced and crushed and expelled and destroyed; persecuted, burned and drowned, and who, despite their anger and their fury, continues to live and to flourish. What is this Jew whom they have never succeeded in enticing with all the enticements in the world, whose oppressors and persecutors only suggested that he deny (and disown) his religion and cast aside the faithfulness of his ancestors?! The Jew - is the symbol of eternity. ... He is the one who for so long had guarded the prophetic message and transmitted it to all mankind. A people such as this can never disappear. The Jew is eternal. He is the embodiment of eternity.
>
> —Leo Tolstoy[197]

> I marvel at the resilience of the Jewish people.
>
> —Elie Wiesel[198]

The miracle of Israel's rebirth is not just that a dispersed and persecuted people miraculously returned to their Promised Land and a nation was born in a day but that a nation demonstrates to the world resilience second-to-none. Rebbetzin Dena Weinberg said, "There are no problems, only opportunities for growth."[199] Rabbi Schneur Zalman of Liadi said, "A little bit of light pushes away a whole lot of darkness."[200]

## Israel's Resilient Democracy

A nation of survivors will create a nation that survives and a resilient people will become a resilient nation. Resilience is in the fabric of Israeli DNA and is on display for all to see. Israel's governance is one of the most resilient in the world. She is the only stable democracy in a region of totalitarian and unstable governments.

While living under constant military and terrorist threat and endless cries for her destruction, Israel has never once succumbed to the wartime pressures that often crush democracies yet belongs to a select group of democracies that has never had a period of undemocratic governance. On the contrary, conflicts and threats have only served to harden Israel's resolve to afford equal rights to all citizens. Even Arabs living in Israel while denying the state's legitimacy and seeking her demise are treated the same as everyone else.

Israel has tolerated actions that would be deemed treasonous in any other democracy. What other democratic nation would uphold the immunity of legislators who praise the terrorists sworn to destroy it? Yet that is exactly what happens, according to Lahav Harkov, the *Jerusalem Post*'s Knesset reporter. On January 18, 2012, he reported that Balad members of the Knesset praised the actions of terrorists, while visiting their families.[201]

> A video purportedly shot at a Palestinian Authority event honouring Palestinian martyrs last week shows MK Ahmed Tibi [a former advisor Yasser Arafat] saying that "there is no greater source of praise" than martyrdom.
>
> While the word martyr in Arabic means to die in the name of God, in the Palestinian-Israeli conflict it has come to be associated with suicide bombers and terrorists who are killed while attacking Israel.[202]

Ahmed Tibi not only remains a member of the Knesset to this day but serves as one of the deputy speakers of Parliament. Israel's democratic credentials were further enhanced when a Likud member the Knesset, MK Zeev Elkin, suggested the members of Tibi's Joint List party had "the blood of the murdered" on their hands.[203,204] Tibi, using his position as a deputy speaker, demanded an apology. Elkin refused and was suspended from Parliament.[205]

Just two weeks later, Tibi was suspended by the Ethics Committee for two weeks, following a petition by Elkin over his suspension. To me, this shows that despite continual attacks on her sovereignty, Israel's parliamentary democracy remains incredibly resilient.

Following more of Balad's Knesset members visiting, consoling and praising terrorist and suicide bombers, Netanyahu quiet reasonably said they didn't deserve to sit in the Knesset, but because Israel, unlike all her neighbours, is a democracy, it was made clear that,

> [the speaker of the Knesset] does not have the authority to punish the Balad MKs, but if the Ethics Committee determines the visit was a violation, it can sanction them with suspensions of up to six months from all Knesset activity but voting—a punishment Zoabi received in the past for comments sympathizing with Hamas during Operation Protective Edge - or a new punishment that has yet to be used, docking their salaries. In addition, if the attorney-general finds their actions to be criminal, he may ask the Knesset House Committee to vote to remove their immunity, so they can be put on trial.[206]

Hanin Zoabi retained her seat and parliamentary immunity. Israeli Arab parties routinely call for dismantling the Jewish state, yet only one party has ever banned from participating in Israeli elections. That was the Kach Party, a Jewish party that preached hatred of Arabs. In their manifesto, Kach wants (1) all Arabs be expelled from the country, to prevent them becoming a majority; (2) the Israeli response to acts of terror to be counter-terror; and (3) the two mosques removed from the Temple Mount. Kach was disqualified by the Central Elections Committee from running in the Eleventh Knesset elections. However, the High Court of Justice ruled that the disqualification was illegal. What other democracy would allow supporters of groups with charters to overthrow the government to sit in and vote in the Parliament?

As with everything to do with Israel, there are critics of her democracy. There are claims that she seeks to limit free speech and violate human rights. The most scathing criticism of Israeli democracy stems from the situation in the West Bank, where the Arabs create the illusion that the democratic values in Israel are being eroded.

But is this justified? Is Israel's democracy truly in jeopardy, and will it retain its character as both a Jewish and a democratic state, a democratic stronghold of stability in the Middle East? Are basic liberties and gender equality in peril?

When Zionism emerged at the end of the nineteenth century, the Jews of Palestine and the thousands who joined them from Russia and from the Middle East had little or no experience of democracy. Communism, brought into Palestine from Eastern Europe as reflected in the form of kibbutz, settlements, and labour unions, had greater influence on early Jewish thought than beacons of democracy in the United States and Britain. Yet from the start, the Jews of the fledgling nation gravitated toward democracy. Intensely ideological and diverse, the Zionist parties—socialist, religious, and nationalist—were forced to work together in the quest for Jewish statehood.

Democratic principles were well established in their psyche long before Israel's declaration of independence on May 14, 1948. Enshrined in the declaration is the guarantee that all citizens will enjoy social and political rights, irrespective of religion, race, or sex. It guarantees freedom of religion, conscience, language, education, and culture.

> Israel had forged the Middle East's first genuinely functional democracy. But the obstacles confronting that system—domestic and external—remained immense. A nation founded by pioneers from autocratic societies would have to wrestle with identity and security issues that would daunt even the most deeply rooted democracies, especially as it subsequently absorbed nearly two million immigrants from the Middle East and the former Soviet bloc. Indeed, in the annals of modern democracy, Israel is entirely unique.[207]

Again, Ayeen Hirsi Ali said,

> My main impression was that Israel is a liberal democracy. In the places I visited, including Jerusalem as well as Tel Aviv and its beaches, I saw that men and women are equal.[208]

The Jewish state is exceptional and its democracy unique. It is a nation-state much like Australia, but it also includes a large minority, the Arabs, whose distinct national and linguistic character is officially recognised.

As far as religion goes, although Judaism has a prominent place in both public and political life, Israel does not have a national religion; rather, it recognises all three monotheistic religions. Israel isn't just home to Jews. Non-Jews account for more than 20 per cent of the population, and each enjoys autonomy in religious affairs and supervises its own sacred places. The greatest example of this is the holiest site in Judaism, the Temple Mount, which is also revered by Muslims and has remained under the auspices of the Islamic *waqf*.[209]

Israel has been criticised for its migration policy, namely the "Law of Return," assuring citizenship to Jewish immigrants. However, many countries have similar laws, and Jews see the law as righting the historic wrong of statelessness that has seen far too many Jewish people suffer persecution and loss in so many countries.

In an opinion, United States Supreme Court Justice William Brennan observed when he visited Israel in 1988,

> It may well be Israel, not the United States that provides the best hope for building a jurisprudence that can protect civil liberties against the demands of national security. For it is Israel that has been facing real and serious threats to its security [since 1948] and seems destined to continue facing such threats in the foreseeable future. The struggle to establish civil liberties against the backdrop of these security threats, while difficult, promises to build bulwarks of liberty that can endure the fears and frenzy of sudden danger—bulwarks to help guarantee that a nation fighting for its survival does not sacrifice those national values that make the fight worthwhile.[210]

In the face of seventy years of hostility, Israel remains a shining beacon of democracy, with tolerant and resilient political and legal systems.

Clearly, Israeli democracy is distinctive, capable of bearing unparalleled burdens and coping with great complexities.

## Conclusion

Ezekiel's prophetic word was that God was bringing His people home, they would come home a people "as good as dead." They came through the holocaust only to be faced with extinction from a Muslim confederacy, determined to finish what Hitler started. Instead of extinction, they have shown great resolve and resilience.

These tendons are what attaches muscle to the bone Israel. We will see in the next chapter that she has developed her muscle! Through her resilience, Israel has thrived and grown into an international powerhouse.

Truly tendons have attached to the bones.

# CHAPTER 10
## Ezekiel—Flesh (Israel's Muscle)

*If the Arabs were to lay down their guns tomorrow, there would be no war. If Israel were to lay down theirs, there would be no Israel.*

—Benjamin Netanyahu

In the previous sections, we saw that universal hatred and anti-Semitism drove the desire for a Jewish homeland. We are not just seeing Jews but the *whole house of Israel* returning to the land God promised to give to Abraham, Isaac, and Israel.[211] In the previous chapter, we saw that tendons serve two biological purposes: they hold bones together and give resilience to the skeleton. All returning Israelis embrace Israeli culture, which holds the nation together. Israel's governance demonstrates a national resilience that is second to none in the Middle East. Despite overwhelming odds, the bones are coming together, and Israel's resilient governance and culture are holding the nation together.

> I will attach tendons to you and make flesh come upon you and cover you with skin; I will put breath in you, and you will come to life. Then you will know that I am the Lord. (Ezekiel 37:6)

Flesh and muscle in this prophecy are synonymous. In this chapter, we will look at the growth of the state of Israel into an international powerhouse. The broken people that began to migrate to Palestine from Europe after World War 2 were never destined to remain broken. God commanded Ezekiel to prophesy a second time. When he did, the whole hose of Israel lived, and stood upon their feet, *an exceedingly great army.* (Ezekiel 37:10)

The nation that was as good as dead when they began to return home had a promise. The dry dead bones would become an exceeding great army. Biologically, tendons also attach muscle to bone. That same resilience that we spoke of in chapter 9 is what has enabled Israel to become strong. The German philosopher Friedrich Nietzsche said, "That which does not kill us makes us stronger." That is so true of Israel. For thousands of years, nations have sought to destroy her, but they have failed miserably, and today Israel grows stronger.

Benjamin Netanyahu, in a speech to the United Nations in September 2016, said,

> More and more nations in Asia, in Africa, in Latin America, more and more nations see Israel as a potent partner—a partner in fighting the terrorism of today, a partner in developing the technology of tomorrow.[212]

As well being a major world power in fighting terrorism and in the development of new and world changing technologies, Netanyahu said that Israel is fast becoming a key diplomatic player on the world stage.

> Today Israel has diplomatic relations with over 160 countries. That's nearly double the number that we had when I served here as Israel's ambassador some 30 years ago.[213] And those ties are getting broader and deeper every day. World leaders increasingly appreciate that Israel is a powerful country with one of the best intelligence services on earth. Because of our unmatched experience and proven capabilities in fighting terrorism, many of your governments seek our help in keeping your countries safe. Many also seek to benefit from Israel's ingenuity in agriculture, in health, in water, in cyber and in the fusion of big data, connectivity and artificial intelligence—that fusion that is changing our world in every way.[214]

Despite rampant and state-sponsored anti-Semitism, Israel has steadily improved her international standing and has become a leader in research and development. Netanyahu spoke of Israel's leadership in wastewater recycling:

> We recycle about 90 per cent of our wastewater. Now, how remarkable is that? Well, given that the next country on the list only recycles about 20 per cent of its wastewater, Israel is a global water power. So, if you have a thirsty world, and we do, there's no better ally than Israel.[215]

Regarding cyber security, Netanyahu said,

> Israel accounts for one-tenth of one percent of the world's population, yet last year we attracted some 20 per cent of the global private investment in cybersecurity. I want you to digest that number. In cyber, Israel is punching a whopping 200 times above its weight. So Israel is also a global cyber power.[216]

Towards the end of what was a remarkable speech, Netanyahu spoke of his boundless optimism for the future:

> I am filled with hope because Israel is capable of defending itself by itself against any threat. I am filled with hope because the valour of our fighting men and women is second to none. I am filled with hope because I know the forces of civilization will ultimately triumph over the forces of terror. I am filled with hope because in the age of innovation, Israel—the innovation nation—

is thriving as never before. I am filled with hope because Israel works tirelessly to advance equality and opportunity for all its citizens: Jews, Muslims, Christians, Druze, everyone. And I am filled with hope because despite all the naysayers, I believe that in the years ahead, Israel will forge a lasting peace with all our neighbours.[217]

## National Power Index

Was Netanyahu's boundless optimism well founded? Was he exaggerating when he described Israel as a potent partner, a global power, and a world leader? Did he overstate Israel's international muscle at the UN? The National Power Index (NPI) is a global survey that compares a nation's strength with that of all other nations. The NPI is a measure of a nation's ability to influence global events. The ranking is based on a country's economy, military, diplomacy, technology, and population. In the 2013 survey, Israel was ranked among the world's ten most powerful countries. This was extraordinary for a country of just 8,000,000 and a land size of 22,000 km². In the latest survey, released in March 2017, Israel was still ranked in the top ten most powerful nations. This is a clear fulfilment of Ezekiel's prophecy that a people who were as good as dead would rise to be a powerful nation.

## NPI—Israel's Economic Capability (Ranked 25th in the World)[218]

The strength of Israel's economy is seen in the markets. In May 2016, there were eighty-one Israeli companies listed on the NASDAQ stock exchange, more than both Germany and Britain, while China, the most populous and fastest-growing world economy, has 117 companies listed. The majority are in the technology and health sectors.

Israel's economic strength was also evident during the Global Financial Crisis. While all other Western economies contracted sharply, Israel's grew by 1.3 per cent in 2009. This was due to structural differences from other Western nations in the Israeli economy. The country's banks are all well capitalised and steep deposit requirements for prospective new homeowners prevent the creation of debt issues that characterised the housing market in the United States.

In 2015, David Walzer, the head of mission of Israel to the EU, was asked to comment on Israel's economic growth, which in 2014 was better than most Western economies. He said,

> I think that [the figures] are even more impressive taking into account the fact that last summer we had a military campaign in Gaza. That meant for almost two months the State of Israel committed a lot of resources into this campaign. Economic activity suffered a substantial

slowdown but it still managed to grow very significantly.[219]

In 2016, the OECD ranked Israel's economy as the thirty-fifth largest economy, a significant result for such a small nation that was on a war footing for most of the year. Also, they battled a worldwide and ill-informed anti-Semitic program known as "Boycott, Divestment, and Sanctions" (BDS), which seeks to undermine her economy.

How has Israel successfully fireproofed her economy? The cliché "necessity is the mother of all invention" is very true of the Israeli economy. Because of the lack of a sizable domestic market, Israeli companies have no choice but to develop strong export markets.

With more than half the world's Jews living outside of Israel, the natural networks that exist made the transition from a net import to an export economy relatively easy. Until recently, Israel was an agricultural economy. Her small land size mass meant that Israel needed to change if it was to become an export economy. With one the most diverse and well educated labour forces in the world, she would not find this problematic. Israel has transitioned well from an agrarian economy to one of the most innovative economies in the world. The OECD has made it clear that the strength of Israel's economy is in her ability to build on its world standing as one of the most innovative economies in the world.

We have yet to mention the most significant reason for the strength of the Jewish economy. God said to Abraham, "Wa·'ă·ḇā·reḵ·kā" ("And I will bless"). This Hebrew word resonates all the way throughout Israel's history. Abraham's son, Isaac, was in conflict with the surrounding nations because they envied the fact that he was greatly blessed in a year of famine. So it is today; Israel has been blessed and the nations that surround her envy her. Add to that the first conflict Israel was involved in was in Egypt, when they were enslaved. After four hundred years they escaped, but not empty handed; they left Egypt with great wealth.

## NPI—Israel's Technology Capability (Ranked 4th in the World)

The World Economic Forum's annual Global Competitiveness Report confirmed what the OECD reports continue to assert, that Israel's strength lies in its innovation. In 2014-15, Israel was third, behind Finland and Switzerland for innovation. This was significantly above both Japan and USA.

Israeli companies have also been very successful in turning geographical and geopolitical challenges to its commercial advantage, with Israel at the forefront of areas such as cyber security and wastewater recycling and desalination.

Israel is the second most educated country in the world, with 46 per cent of twenty-five to sixty-four-year-olds having a tertiary qualification.[220] This reflects the importance Israel places on science and technology. Israel also has the highest percentage in the world of home computers per capita.[221] With such a well-educated and tech-savvy population, it is not surprising that Israel leads the world in the number of scientists and technicians in the workforce.[222]

## Research and Development

With Innovation comes Research and Development (R&D). You cannot have one without the other and Israel is ranked the second top nation worldwide behind South Korea in R&D as a percentage of GDP in the world.[223]

Netanyahu, in his speech, referred to Israel's small population despite its huge impact on R&D, reminding the world that a nation that makes up one-tenth of 1 per cent of the world's population has a whopping 20 per cent of the global investment in cyber security.[224] With a population of less than 500,000, Tel Aviv is known as one of the most technologically influential cities in the world. There are more than 250 foreign R&D companies located in Israel, while Yokneam, in northern Israel, with a population of just over 21,000, is home to more than one hundred high-tech and R&D companies.

Israel's R&D covers a broad range of fields, including agriculture, computer sciences, electronics, genetics, health care, optics, green technologies, and engineering.

## Green Technology

The Global Cleantech Innovation Index explores which countries currently have the greatest potential to produce entrepreneurial clean-tech start-ups that will commercialise clean technology innovations over the next ten years.[225] The most recent index and its accompanying report were released in 2014, and Israel was ranked number one. We will look at that in detail in the next chapter.

## Computer Hardware, Software, and Cell Phones

There are also many computer and phone companies with R&D centres in Israel, employing thousands of people. Among the computer giants in Israel are Microsoft, Dell, EMC, HP, IBM, Apple, Lenovo, LG, Samsung, and Xiaomi.

## Microsoft

Software giant Microsoft has three R&D centres in Israel employing more than 1,000 people. The company's R&D centres in Israel are among the few development centres they have outside the US. Zack Weisfeld, the head of Microsoft Global Accelerators said,

> There is something about the culture, and something about the market understanding and business understanding that might be a little rougher [among Israeli startups] at the beginning, but at the end of the day, and if you get them to the right place, they're unstoppable.[226]

In a February speech broadcast at Microsoft Israel's annual Think Next event, Microsoft founder Bill Gates said that Israeli contributions to technology fields such as analytics and security are "improving the world."

## Google

Google first opened its Tel Aviv office in 2006 and now employs more than 600 Israeli engineers, who work on their core products.

Don Dodge from Google, who travels the world talking to developers and investors, said,

> I've been to every corner of the earth. China, Japan, Australia, all of Europe, the Nordics, everywhere. There is no other country on earth that thinks the same way that we [Google] do like Israel does. Israel truly is the "Startup Nation." You think like us. You break things, you make things and you're creative. It's special.[227]

"There's an amazing source of talent here," Dodge said. "It's about innovation, creativity, taking tremendous risks, understanding how to get to market. That's what Israel does. It's not about the cost."[228]

In 2013, Google purchased the Israeli navigation app Waze for $1.3 billion, at the time the largest-ever deal for an app.

Eric Schmidt, executive chairman of Google's parent company Alphabett said,

> For a relatively small country, Israel has a super role in global technological innovation," I can't think of a place where you could see this diversity and the collection of initiatives aside from Silicon Valley. That is a pretty strong statement.[229]

## Facebook

Similarly, when Adi Soffer Teeni, the CEO of Facebook Israel, was asked what distinguished Israel as a tech hub, she pointed to the local talent. According to Teeni, Facebook's engineering team in Israel was key to developing one of the social media network's latest products.[230]

"There's amazing talent here. Multinationals come here with great R&D centres and recruit people with a very innovative way of thinking."[231]

She added that the culture in Facebook's R&D facility in Israel, which opened three years ago, was similar to that of its Silicon Valley R&D facility, where workers "move fast and break things" while wearing "shorts and flip-flops."

"Something is happening here in Israel," she said. "There's a magic and it's not easy to explain what it is, but Israel's a playground where it feels like home for the multinational."[16]

## Intel

Ray Ramon, managing director of Intel's Ingenuity Partner Program, said his company was one of Israel's biggest employers, with some 11,000 workers across the nation.

The micro processing giant's first Israeli branch, which opened in 1974, was also its first design and development hub outside of the United States.

Ramon spoke of Israeli *chutzpah*, which he called a useful tool that helps Israelis approach business ventures with boldness and confidence.[232]

> "The reason I started the startup program is because when you meet with a company in Israel, they come in and tell engineers that they're doing it all wrong," he said. "They push everything off the table. These engineers have been doing this for years. They're world experts. And yet that startup is bold enough to come to a mammoth like Intel and say you're doing it all wrong. This is one culture that you can't get anywhere in the world."[233]

Intel's main development centre in Israel has been credited with some of the microprocessor giant's most advanced products. Intel's newest core processor chip, Kaby Lake, was built by the company's team in Haifa. Intel has produced and exported more than one billion processors from Israel, including the 8088, which was the first processor developed for personal computers, and the Pentium MMX, which was the most popular processor in the twentieth century.

## NPI—Israel's Military Capability (Ranked 6th in the World)

American President Harry Truman knew Israel was in awful trouble in the months following the United Nations vote to create a Jewish homeland. She was surrounded by hostile Arab nations that made no secret of its intent to invade the moment the British withdrew.

Though he understood the mood of the Arabs and the threat to Israel, Truman didn't want to be seen to take sides, so he enforced an arms embargo on both the Arabs and Jews. Truman saw this as the United States being diplomatic, but this opinion was incredibly naive. The Arabs had at their disposal an arsenal of British weapons and intelligence, while the Jews were forced to smuggle weapons from Eastern Europe, principally from Czechoslovakia. The first shipment arrived on the March 31 and consisted of two hundred rifles, forty MG-34 machine guns, and bullets. A second shipment, of forty-five hundred rifles and two hundred machine guns, along with ammunition, arrived at a Tel Aviv port on April 2, hidden among fresh fruit and vegetables. Finally, a third shipment arrived on the April 28, sixteen days before independence, consisting of 10,000 rifles, 1,415 machine guns, and bullets.[234]

On May 15, the day after Israel declared independence, five Arab states invaded and Israel was plunged into a war that lasted more than a year. At the outbreak of hostilities, Israel's army had no cannons or tanks, and its entire air force consisted of nine obsolete WW2 planes. Although the Haganah had 60,000 trained fighters, fewer than 19,000 were fully mobilised and prepared for war.[235,236] Despite overwhelming odds, at the end of the War of Independence, more land was under Israeli control than when the Arab nations invaded. This was a great miracle.

Building on a foundation of pre-independence militias and cast-off WWII weapons, the IDF has continued to enjoy remarkable success in the field. The balance of military power in the Middle East has shifted dramatically since the War of Independence. The 2016 Global Firepower Report ranked Israel's military sixteenth in the world. Its army has 4,000 tanks, 10,000 Armoured Vehicles, and 3 million men and women (38 per cent of the total population) fit for service and a navy with forty-six coastal defence craft and six submarines.[237] As for the IAF (Israeli Air Force), it has 680 planes. Christopher Harmer, a senior naval analyst with the Middle East Security Project, says, "Pilot to pilot, airframe to airframe, the Israeli air force is the best in the world."[238] Finally, the 2013 NPI report deemed Israel's military capability sixth in the world. What an amazing transformation in less than seventy years.

The *Haaretz News*, on Oct 28, 2014, reported,

> Israel has a qualitative edge over the region, thanks to a close defence relationship with the U.S. and its own defence industry. This edge includes space assets, advanced fighter jets, drones, and nuclear weapons.[239]

In the 1960s and 1970s, because of its unique needs and problems associated with on-again-off-again international boycotts, Israel saw the need to develop a state-of-the-art defence industry. As a direct result, Israel boasts one of the most technologically advanced military stockpiles in the world and one of the world's most effective military workforces. In 2014, the Stockholm International Peace Research Institute Index (SIPRI) ranked three Israeli companies, Israel Aerospace Industries, Elbit Systems, and RAFAEL, in the top sixty military weapons producers and military service companies worldwide.[240,241]

Since 1948, the state of Israel has built an effective military machine. Here are five examples of Israel's *home-grown* military might.

1. Merkava

The Merkava Tank, designed and built in Israel, overcomes obstacles of supply and the uniqueness of the Israeli terrain. They have been continually modified to reflect the changes in conflicts. The IDF have been using an updated Merkava IV in the conflicts in Gaza to penetrate Palestinian positions while keeping IDF soldiers safe. Around 1,600 Merkavas of various types have been in service since the late 1970s.

2. F-15I Thunder

The Israeli Air Force has flown variants of the F-15 since the 1970s. The F-15I thunder can hit targets with precision at long range and is far superior to the aircraft available to Israel's sworn enemies. Israel now has the most lethal squadron of aircraft in the Middle East. Most analysts expect that the F-15I would play a key role in any Israeli strike against Iran.

3. F-21 Kfir

Israel Aerospace Industries manufactures and exports the F-21 Kfir a single-seat multitask fighter plane that can fly at an altitude of 30,000 m, with a range of 1,300 km at speeds more than 2,200 km/h.

The US Navy and Marine Corps are so impressed by the Kfir's capabilities that they have leased several fighters.

4. Jericho III

The earliest Israeli nuclear deterrent came in the form of the F-4 Phantom fighter-bombers that the IAF used to great effect in the War of Attrition and the Yom Kippur War.[242] As the Arabs acquired more sophisticated missiles, Israel saw the need for a more effective and secure deterrent and began to invest heavily in ballistic missile technology. The Jericho I ballistic missile entered service in the early 1970s, and it was eventually replaced by the Jericho II and Jericho III.

The Jericho III is the most advanced ballistic missile in the region, capable of striking targets not only in the Middle East but also across Europe, Asia, and even as far as North America.

The Jericho III ensures that any nuclear attack against Israel would be met with devastating retaliation, especially as it is unlikely that Israel could be disarmed by a first strike. Of course, given that no potential Israeli foe has nuclear weapons (or will have them in the next decade, at least), the missiles give Jerusalem presumptive nuclear superiority across the region.

5. Namer Armored Personnel Carrier

Most infantry fighting vehicles are not heavily armoured and are susceptible to attack from tank rounds and anti-tank guided missiles. This really is bizarre, considering infantry fighting vehicles fight alongside the much more heavily armoured tanks.

The Namer is different, having been built from the obsolete Merkava I tank. Having removed the turret and main gun, Israel was able to add a significant amount of armour without adding to the overall weight of the original Merkava tanks. About 120 Merkavas have been converted into Namers, enough to equip about three battalions.

Namer has a crew of three, including driver, remote weapons station operator, and commander. It can carry nine infantrymen.

## NPI—Foreign Affairs Capability (Ranked 19th in the World)

Israel has a huge influence in the Middle East region, with the strongest military in the area and the most stable government. Despite hate-filled rhetoric, many nations seek to normalise relations with Israel. As of 2017, 158 countries have diplomatic relations with Israel, far more than do not. Of those countries, there are 79 embassies, 22 are consulates, and 6 are special missions throughout the world.

Despite the blatant bias of the UN against Israel's interests, Israel maintains a mission to the United Nations (New York), a mission to the United Nations institutions in Geneva, Paris, and Vienna, and a mission to the European Union (Brussels).

Netanyahu's speech to the UN opened with this:

> Mr President, Ladies and Gentlemen, What I'm about to say is going to shock you: Israel has a bright future at the UN. Now I know that hearing that from me must surely come as a surprise, because year after year I've stood at this very podium and slammed the UN for its obsessive bias against Israel. And the UN deserved every scathing word—for the disgrace of the General Assembly that last year passed 20 resolutions against the democratic State of Israel and a grand total of three resolutions against all the other countries on the planet.[243]

After the scathing opening remarks, Netanyahu concluded his opening comments with a note of optimism:

> So when it comes to Israel at the UN, you'd probably think nothing will ever change, right? Well think again. You see, everything will change and a lot sooner than you think. The change will happen in this hall, because back home, your governments are rapidly changing their attitudes towards Israel. And sooner or later, that's going to change the way you vote on Israel at the UN.[244]

His optimism is borne out by the by the increase in Israel's influence throughout the world, particularly by its leadership in research and development which aids not only Israel but the world.

## NPI—Population Capability (Ranked 17th in the World)

NPI's population capability is not a measure of the size of a population; rather, it looks at all aspects of the population. Israel's population is not large, but it is highly educated and relatively young, and surprisingly, life expectancy in Israel is higher than in both the United States and Australia.

When looking at the population, NPI considers the percentage of men and women trained for the military, and the tiny nation of Israel has one of the world's highest percentage of men and women in the military.

Another report to consider when looking at the men and women of Israel is the "World Happiness Report," which was commissioned the United Nations to help guide their public policies. The report is a survey of 158 nations and looks at their overall well-being, ranking "happiness" levels using similar criteria as NPI as well as considering factors such as social support, generosity, freedom to make life choices, and the perception of government corruption.

It is staggering that a nation that lives daily under the threat of terrorism and has suffered so much hostility throughout the ages has been ranked the eleventh happiest nation in the world, just below Australia and New Zealand but above the United States.[245]

What makes Israelis happy?

Psychologist Tal Ben-Shahar believes it has nothing to do with the geographical location and everything to do with the people inside this tiny nation. He said, "It's because of our focus on relationships. Friends and family are very high up on our value scale, and quality time with them is given a priority. Time we spend with people we care about and who care about us is the number one predictor of happiness."[246]

The Jews are quick to remind the rest of the world that Israel is never boring, and the people don't take themselves too seriously.

## NPI—Energy Security (Ranked 26th in the World)

Just fifteen years ago, Israel relied entirely on imported coal, natural gas, and oil for its energy needs. It imported much of the oil and gas from Egypt, but repeated attacks on the pipelines made this a major problem. Israel's solution was to become energy independent.

She went in search of alternative energy sources, and in 2009 she found gas in the Tamar natural gas field, off the Mediterranean Coast. Tamar now produces 1.2 billion cubic feet of gas a day, enough for 40 per cent of Israel's power generation.

In 2011, two energy companies, the US-based Noble Energy and Israel's Delek, discovered the Leviathan field. Until recently, it was the largest gas field ever discovered in the Mediterranean. It contains an estimated 22 trillion cubic feet of gas. In addition, Israel has discovered large oil deposits in the disputed Golan Heights.

Israel is expected to become an energy exporter by the end of this decade, and the government is planning to establish a sovereign wealth fund to ensure that the windfall proceeds from this unexpected source of public revenue are wisely invested.

## Conclusion

One of the most amazing miracles of the last one hundred years is how Israel has transformed herself into one of the most powerful nations in the world, despite its small size and population and being on a constant war footing against the surrounding nations and terrorist within determined to see her crushed.

The last word should go to Netanyahu, from his UN speech:

> Governments are changing their attitudes towards Israel because they know that Israel can help them protect their peoples, can help them feed them, can help them better their lives … I am hopeful about what Israel can accomplish because I've seen what Israel has accomplished. In 1948, the year of Israel's independence, our population was 800,000. Our main export was oranges. People said then we were too small, too weak, too isolated, too demographically outnumbered to survive, let alone thrive. The sceptics were wrong about Israel then; the septics are wrong about Israel now … Israel's population has grown tenfold, our economy fortyfold. Today our biggest export is technology—Israeli technology, which powers the world's computers, cell phones, cars and so much more.[22]

Muscle is forming on the bones before our very eyes.

## Postscript

In March 2017, it was reported in the *Haaretz News* that Israel remains in the top ten most powerful nations in the world.[247]

# CHAPTER 11
## Ezekiel—Skin (Israel's Beautiful Land)

*In the tradition of the early Zionist pioneers, Jewish farmers continue to use a mixture of hard work and innovation to make Israel "a land of milk and honey."*

—Israel's Ministry for Foreign Affairs

*The wilderness and dry land will be glad. The desert will rejoice and blossom like a lily.*

—Isaiah 35:1 TLV

In the previous chapters, we have seen that Jews and *the whole house of Israel* have been returning from all corners of the globe to their promised land. We saw that the state of Israel was born in a day. And we saw that Israel in just seventy years has grown into an international powerhouse. All three are fulfilments of Old Testament prophecies.

> I will attach tendons to you and make flesh come upon you and cover you with skin; I will put breath in you, and you will come to life. Then you will know that I am the Lord ... I looked, and tendons and flesh appeared on them and skin covered them, but there was no breath in them. (Ezekiel 37:6, 8)

There remains one more aspect of Ezekiel's prophecy that is being fulfilled today. He said that God was going to cover Israel with skin. To the Old Testament prophets, skin spoke of beauty. Ezekiel saw the day when Israel would be beautified. However, not only Ezekiel but all the Old Testament prophets who saw the day when the land would be transformed. In this chapter, we will see the transformation of the land. Since 1948 what has been happening to the land of Israel is a miracle of Biblical proportions and further proof that God's covenant with Abraham, Isaac and Israel is still valid today.

David Walzer, Head of Mission of Israel to the EU, says that Israel is "small but beautiful. It is probably one of the only places in the world where in winter you can start your day skiing on the Golan Heights and within a few hours be swimming in the Dead Sea."[248]

Around 3,500 years ago, God appeared to Moses and told him that He was freeing Israel from 400 years of slavery and bringing them to a good land that flowed with milk and honey.[249]

Centuries later God described Israel to the prophet Amos. Amos prophesied judgment on Israel's neighbours then turned his attention to a coming judgement on Judah (the Jews) and Jerusalem and finally the judgement that would soon fall on Israel (the ten tribes of the divided kingdom). Judgement, judgement, judgement, and then, as if completely out of place, Amos prophesies the future restoration Israel.[250]

The restoration of Israel has four interconnected promises:

1. Israel would be fruitful and productive.
2. The returning exiles would rebuild and live in the ruined cities.
3. Israel would have a self-sufficient economy.
4. Israel would never again be exiled from their land.

We will now turn our attention to seeing how these promises are being fulfilled before our eyes.

## Promise 1: A Fruitful and Productive Land

"Behold, the days are coming," says the Lord,
"When the ploughman shall overtake the reaper,
And the treader of grapes him who sows seed;
The mountains shall drip with sweet wine,
And all the hills shall flow with it." (Amos 9:13)

Amos sees a time when the Land of Israel will be such a productive land that farmers will have hardly finished breaking up the ground for planting when the crops would be ready for harvesting. The crops produced will be so abundant and grow so quickly that there will not be time to crush the grapes from one harvest before the next seasons grapes are ready for harvesting.

Despite this promise, when the nation was born in 1948, Israel was not a land flowing with milk and honey; rather, it was a veritable wasteland.

Mark Twain visited Palestine in 1867 and described it as follows:

> [A] desolate country whose soil is rich enough, but is given over wholly to weeds - a silent mournful expanse. ... A desolation is here that not even imagination can grace with the pomp of life and action. ... We never saw a human being on the whole route. ... There was hardly a tree or a shrub anywhere. Even the olive and the cactus, those fast friends of the worthless soil, had

almost deserted the country.[251]

Mark Twain noticed the soil was rich enough but had been neglected.
The Report of the Palestine Royal Commission in 1913, described the coastal road from Gaza northward as follows:

> [O]nly a summer track suitable for transport by camels and carts ... no orange groves, orchards or vineyards were to be seen until one reached [the Jewish village of] Yabna [Yavne]. ... Houses were all of mud. No windows were anywhere to be seen. ... The ploughs used were of wood. ... The yields were very poor. ... The sanitary conditions in the village were horrible. Schools did not exist. ... The western part, towards the sea, was almost a desert. ... The villages in this area were few and thinly populated. Many ruins of villages were scattered over the area, as owing to the prevalence of malaria, many villages were deserted by their inhabitants.[252]

The British in 1917 described Palestine as inadequate to form a home for either the Jewish or any other people and incapable of sustaining the certain increase of Jewish migration if they were granted Palestine as a homeland.[253]

Secretary of State Lord Balfour countered the War Cabinet's pessimism by making the following argument:

> With regard to the [inadequacy of Palestine to become a Jewish homeland], [Balfour] understood that there were considerable differences of opinion among experts regarding the possibility of the settlement of any large population in Palestine, but he was informed that, if Palestine were scientifically developed, a very much larger population could be sustained than had existed during the period of Turkish misrule.[254]

What Mark Twain noticed and Balfour believed was that the land was good enough but was suffering from centuries of Arab neglect.

A neglected land was not the biggest obstacle facing Palestine. A report commissioned by the British in 1921 concluded that malaria stood out as the worst disease in Palestine; it had decimated the population for centuries and was the largest hindrance to farming large areas of fertile lands.[255] Malaria was such a problem in Palestine that in 1902, all the Turkish soldiers at a border post were rotated home monthly; otherwise, everyone would contract malaria in a week. In 1917, when Britain liberated Palestine from the centuries of Ottoman neglect, they described the land as "notoriously malarious," and an estimated 90 per cent of British soldiers at the town of Beisan were struck down with malaria within ten days.[256]

It seemed the Palestine landscape was a picture of two extremes, either deserts or malaria infested swamplands, and the Arabs were happy to sell the malaria-ridden lowlands to Jewish migrants at highly inflated prices just so they could rid themselves of the problem. The state of the land should have distressed the Jews of the *Aliyah* but they came armed with one of the great promises of scripture that once they began to return the deserts and wastelands would be transformed.

> The wilderness and the wasteland shall be glad for them,
> And the desert shall rejoice and blossom as the rose.
> (Isaiah 35:1)

> For the Lord will comfort Zion,
> He will comfort all her waste places;
> He will make her wilderness like Eden,
> And her desert like the garden of the Lord;
> Joy and gladness will be found in it,
> Thanksgiving and the voice of melody. (Isaiah 51:3)

> The desolate land shall be tilled instead of lying desolate in the sight of all who pass by so they will say, 'This land that was desolate has become like the garden of Eden … (Ezekiel 36:34, 35)

Joels says that wine will flow like rivers from mountains.

> And it will come to pass in that day
> That the mountains shall drip with new wine,
> The hills shall flow with milk,
> And all the brooks of Judah shall be flooded with water;
> A fountain shall flow from the house of the Lord
> And water the Valley of Acacias. (Joel 3:18)

Just like Amos and Ezekiel, Isaiah and Joel saw a day when the land would be transformed and become productive and fruitful again. Isaiah and Ezekiel describe Israel as being "like Eden." For this great promise to be fulfilled, two things needed to happen: malaria needed to be eradicated, and water needed to flow in the deserts.

## *Israel Deals with Malaria and Swamplands*

Israel Jacob Kligler was a little-known Jewish migrant who came to Israel in the early 1920s.[257] His greatest achievement was the eradication of malaria in Palestine. Before 1920, all efforts in dealing with malaria centred on harm minimization, as the prevailing view was that malaria could not be eliminated, only reduced. Kligler established the Malaria Research Institute, which employed hundreds of workers who began to drain swamps and spray areas where they found concentrations of mosquito larvae.

Their research found a variety of innovative ways to eliminate the mosquito population. The results of their work were striking. In 1923, 633 people were treated for malaria in Jerusalem. Twelve months later, that number had dropped to 347, and in 1928, the number was just 16.[258] Kligler did not survive to hear Ben Gurion declare Israel a sovereign nation, but his work proved invaluable. Reporter Matti Friedman in the *Times of Israel*, on April 25, 2012, said, "Israel Kligler is one of the reasons Israel exists."[259]

> Israel Kligler played an [enormous] role in defeating malaria in Palestine beginning in the 1920s. Countering the mosquito-borne disease was not a minor medical success but a crucial victory that paved the way for the growth of Jewish settlement and the eventual establishment of the State of Israel.[260]

At the same time Jews were undertaking major efforts to drain swamps for farming, they planted Australian eucalyptus trees in swamps because they absorb large amounts of water. This helped, but it did not completely solve the problem. Migrants began digging canals to drain the swamps to the sea.

Thanks to Klinger and the hard work and ingenuity of settlers, malaria was eradicated and large areas of swamplands were reclaimed for farming.

## *Israel's Need for Water*

In the regions of Israel, it seemed there was either too much water that needed to be drained or a distinct lack of water. Yet God promised Israel streams, pools, springs, and gushing rivers.

> Then the lame shall leap like a deer,
> And the tongue of the dumb sing.
> For waters shall burst forth in the wilderness,
> And streams in the desert.
> The parched ground shall become a pool,
> And the thirsty land springs of water;
> In the habitation of jackals, where each lay,
> There shall be grass with reeds and rushes.
> A highway shall be there, and a road,
> And it shall be called the Highway of Holiness.
> The unclean shall not pass over it,

> But it shall be for others.
> Whoever walks the road, although a fool,
> Shall not go astray. (Isaiah 35:6–8)
>
> I will open rivers in desolate heights,
> And fountains in the midst of the valleys;
> I will make the wilderness a pool of water,
> And the dry land springs of water.
> I will plant in the wilderness the cedar and the acacia tree,
> The myrtle and the oil tree;
> I will set in the desert the cypress tree and the pine
> And the box tree together,
> That they may see and know,
> And consider and understand together,
> That the hand of the Lord has done this,
> And the Holy One of Israel has created it. (Isaiah 41:18–20)

Israel needs water and lots of it. Yet in the last decade, Israel, like most of the other nations in the Middle East, had to find solutions to water shortages due to the worst drought in more than 900 years.[261]

## Israel Has Become the World Leader in Recycling Wastewater

Netanyahu, in his UN speech, mentioned Israel's advance technology in recycling wastewater. He reminded the UN that Israel recycles 90 per cent of its wastewater, and the next best nation, Spain, only recycles 20 per cent. In a world that the UN says is in desperate need of water, Israel leads the way in recycling.

## Israel Has Become the World Leader in Desalination

Israel is a global water power in the field of desalination thanks to Israel's technological advancements.[262] Desalinisation works by pushing saltwater into membranes containing microscopic pores. The water gets through, while the larger salt molecules are left behind. Unfortunately, microorganisms in seawater can quickly block the pores, and cleaning them requires regular and costly chemical-intensive cleaning. Israel has developed a new chemical-free system using lava stone to capture the microorganisms before they reach the membranes. It's one of many water miracles that allow Israel to obtain 55 per cent of its domestic water from desalination.

## Israel Can Get Water from Thin Air

There is a third way that Israel has solved its water crisis. An Israeli company, Water-Gen, was named one of the World's Fifty Most Innovative Companies.[263] Water-Gen has built machines specifically designed to harvest water vapour from air. Using plastic "leaves" to funnel air in various directions, these water generators appear to create pure drinking water out of nothing.[264] Maxim Pasik, Water-Gen's chairman, said that his company truly believes that it is possible to supply the world with drinking water, and that is the driving force behind Water-Gen.

These three innovations shown that even after continued drought conditions, Israel's water production far surpasses the needs of its eight million citizens. Israel is now able to export water to its neighbours and shares its technology with the world.

## Jewish National Fund (Keren Kayemeth Leisrael)—(JNF-KKL)

Long before private companies developed some amazing technologies to help solve the water crisis, Theodor Herzl was determined a national fund would be established to help Jewish settlers and reclaim the wastelands of Palestine. His dream became a reality in 1901, during the Fifth Zionist Congress in Basel, Switzerland, when the Congress set a goal of raising £200,000. One of the delegates immediately pledged £10. Herzl made the second donation, and his aide the third, and the Jewish National Fund (Keren Kayemeth LeIsrael) (JNF-KKL) was established.

From those humble beginnings more than a century ago, the JNF has worked with other academic and scientific institutions and has become a world leader in environmental action, both in Israel and abroad. They have planted more than 250 million trees, built 240 reservoirs and dams, and developed 250,000 acres of land (5 per cent of Israel), creating 2,000 parks and provided the infrastructure for over 1,000 communities. The JNF still remains the property of the Jewish people.

## Pools in the Desert

The JNF-KKL has built a series of limans in the Negev Desert to fight desertification without depleting groundwater resources. Limans are manmade dunes built to collect floodwater by damming a gully or streambed slowing the flow of the accumulated runoff water, causing it to soak into the soil allowing small groves of trees to flourish in areas with very low rainfall.[265]

## Turning the Desert Green

One of JNF's largest projects is the Yatir Forest. They began planting trees in 1966 with the aim of reducing the size of the Negev Desert. Since then, it has become the largest forest in Israel, completely changing the arid landscape of the northern Negev. The Yatir Forest has not only halted the growth of the Negev Desert but has significantly improved the quality of the air by reducing the amount carbon dioxide levels.

It has taken the word of God, a connection to the land, a century of hard work and water to transform a wilderness into an oasis.

## Making Plants Drought Resistant

As well as turning deserts green and conserving water, Israel is at the forefront of genetically modifying plants to make them drought resistant, even if by accident.

Plant biologist Shimon Gepstein's team at Technion-Israel Institute of Technology were researching the use cytokinins, hoping to extend the growth period and shelf life of tobacco leaves.[266] His staff inadvertently failed to water some of genetically modified plants for several weeks, and surprisingly, after being re-watered, they bounced back to life. Gepstein's team, quite by accident, discovered that adding cytokinin increases a plant's ability to withstand drought.

In Israel, after the first winter rain, seedlings germinate, and if there's no rain for a few weeks, they cannot survive. If genetically modified plants can withstand this dry period until the second rains, whole crops can the saved. Gepstein, while researching ways to delay the aging of plants, ended up with a far more important discovery and one that is of great advantage for Israeli farmers.

His team's breakthrough is benefiting agriculture everywhere, not just in Israel. This breakthrough has shown that these genetically modified food crops require much less water and can be grown in much drier areas that have fewer natural resources.

## Promise 2— The Return of a United Israel and Rebuilding the Ruined Cities

> I will bring back the captives of My people Israel;
> They shall build the waste cities and inhabit them. (Amos 9:14a)

The state of the land should have distressed the Jews of the *Aliyah*, but they came with a promise that once they began returning they would build the waste cities and inhabit them. The transformation of the cities is seen graphically in these photos of Tel Aviv.

Figure 6 - The Dramatic Transformation of Tel Aviv since 1948

On the left is Tel Aviv in 1948, when it became the new nation's capital. On the right is Tel Aviv today.

The Jewish population of Tel Aviv has increased from just 1,500 in 1914 to well over 300,000 today. The Jews have rebuilt the waste city and inhabited it. Tel Aviv's dramatic transformation is confirmed by Lonely Planet, which ranked Tel Aviv in the top three cities in the world in 2010, describing it as follows:[267]

> [M]odern, vibrant and cosmopolitan one of the country's greatest assets, a sun-bronzed strip of coastline where coffee and culinary innovation are the local obsessions, where residents speak every language under the sun, and where life is lived outdoors and to the fullest.[268]

Haifa has also undergone a similar transformation and seen its Jewish population grow from 6,000 in 1920 to over 200,000. While in Jerusalem, the Jewish population has grown from 34,000 in 1922 to over 500,000 today.

Other Jewish cities have seen similar growth and transformations in the last seventy years as Israel has worked tirelessly to see waste cities revived, renewed and rebuilt, and inhabited.

## Promise 3—A Self-Sufficient Economy

> They shall plant vineyards and drink wine from them;

> They shall also make gardens and eat fruit from them. (Amos 9:14b)

Since independence, the total population in Israel has increased from around 1,000,000 to over 8,000,000. The increase was predominately Jewish migration, but the Arab population increased by as much as a million in that time.

Israel is thriving because God promised that they would drink wine from their vineyards and eat fruit from their gardens. Despite the reservations expressed by the British War Council in 1917 concerning Palestine's ability to sustain an increase in population, another miracle has unfolded. In just seventy years, Israel's population has increased eightfold, and she is nearly self-sufficient when it comes to food production. Since 1948, the sparsely populated Negev Desert accounts for more than 40 per cent of the country's vegetables and field crops.[269]

The promises are clear: Israel is a land that flows with milk and honey; wine vats overflow and olive oil in abundance.

## A Land Flowing with Milk and Honey

The prophet Joel said that the mountains shall flow with milk. The *Jerusalem Post* reported June 10, 2011, that

> [l]ocal cows produce the highest amounts of milk per animal in the world, with an average of 10,208 kilograms (around 10,000 litres) of dairy in 2009, according to data published in 2011 by the Israel Central Bureau of Statistics, outperforming cows in the US (9,331 kg (20,571 lb) per cow), Japan (7,497), the European Union (6,139) and Australia (5,601).
>
> A total of 1,304 million litres of milk was produced by Israeli cows in 2010.
>
> All of the Israel's milk consumption originates from dairy farms within the country with most herds consisting largely of Israel-Holsteins, a high-yielding, disease-resistant breed.[270]

Israel is self-sufficient at milk producing enough for the domestic market.

## An Abundance of Olive Oil

Jeremiah prophesied that when Israel returns there would be an abundance of olive oil.[271] The number and size of olive groves in Israel has seen a steep increase and produce between 15,000 and 16,000 tons of extra-virgin olive oil.[272] Israel still needs to import olive oil, as demand outweighs supply, but Israel believes its supply will soon outstrip local demand. In 2014, production met 95 per cent of the demand but fell away in 2015-16.[273] The reason for the reduction in the oil produced was the high costs associated with production and not the quality of the land.[274]

## Vats Overflowing with Wine

Amos said that the Jews would plant vineyards, and Joel prophesied that the mountains shall drip with new wine. The Yatir Forrest is home to the Yatir Winery, situated on a hill 900 meters above sea level. Since 2012, it has produced around 150,000 bottles annually. Another prophetic fulfilment: the mountains that were once nothing more than inhospitable desert land are now home to a highly profitable winery. The owners of the winery have found 180 ancient wine presses, dating back to biblical times. A further sign that God is restoring the land is that vineyards are now being planted upon the very sites of ancient vineyards.

There are now sixty commercial wineries and three hundred wineries in all, and many more domestic or garagiste wineries producing about 40 million bottles of wine and 10 million bottles of grape juice.[275,276]

## Citrus in Abundance

Amos said the Israelis would plant gardens and eat the fruit from them. Could he have possibly imagined the miracle that has unfolded in the last hundred years? The growth of Israel's citrus industry is truly fulfilling Amos' word.

|  | Consumption (Tons) | Production (Metric tons) |
|---|---|---|
| Oranges | 40,000 | 73,000 |
| Grapefruit | 12,000 | 208,000 |
| Mandarins (easy peelers) | 70,000 | 178,000 |
| Lemons/limes | 49.000 | 51.000 |
| Others | 5,000 | 6,000 |
| Total | 176,000 | 517,000 |

Table 11.2 - Comparison of Production and Consuption of Citrus Fruit 2013-14

The table above shows the consumption and production figures for 2013-14, which have not changed significantly for the last decade. It shows that Israel produces two and a half times more citrus than required.

Figs, dates, and pomegranates are all foods that are found in Israel today, which all point to the fulfilment of the promise of self-sufficiency.

The only exception is grain products. Israel imports as much as 95 per cent of the grains, wheat, barley, and corn its people need. Even in that area, Israel's production is increasing.

## Promise 4 – Israel Is In the Land to Stay

> I will plant them in their land,
> And no longer shall they be pulled up
> From the land I have given them,"
> Says the Lord your God. (Amos 9:15)

The final word from God is that never again would Israel be sent into exile; nor would the efforts of her enemies see her driven from the land. We will look at that promise in the last section.

## Conclusion

What an amazing transformation, from shantytowns to the most liveable cities in the Middle East, from a wasteland to a major producer and exporter, and from deserts to forests. All this has occurred in less than one hundred years.

What is striking is that there is no repentance, there is no seeking after God, there is no acceptance of the long-anticipated Messiah. God in His grace and His mercy, and in being faithful to His covenant with Abraham, brings His people home and establishes them in their land! The bones have been rattling and coming together for nearly 150 years, and the nation was reborn in 1948. Since then, God has been adding tendons, flesh, and skin, making Israel a powerful and beautiful nation.

Ezekiel's vision doesn't end at that point. The last thing Ezekiel sees is yet to be fulfilled. Which we will look at in later chapter.

# CHAPTER 12
## Genesis—Blessed to Be a Blessing

*No country in the history of the world has ever contributed more to humankind and accomplished more for its people in so brief a period of time as Israel has done since its relatively recent rebirth in 1948.*

—Alan Dershowitz

> Of Abraham His servant,
> You children of Jacob, His chosen ones!
> He is the Lord our God;
> His judgments are in all the earth.
> He remembers His covenant forever,
> The word which He commanded, for a thousand generations,
> The covenant which He made with Abraham,
> And His oath to Isaac,
> And confirmed it to Jacob for a statute,
> To Israel as an everlasting covenant,
> Saying, "To you I will give the land of Canaan
> As the allotment of your inheritance." (Psalms 105:6–11)

The Psalmist says that God remembers His covenant with Abraham and confirmed it with Israel [Jacob]. Why did God make a covenant with Israel, and why it is important for Him to remember it? The answers are found in the original promise God made to Abraham.

> I will make you a great nation;
> I will bless you
> And make your name great;
> And you shall be a blessing.
> I will bless those who bless you,
> And I will curse him who curses you;
> And in you all the families of the earth shall be blessed." (Genesis 12:2–3)

The covenant contained three promises:

1. As we have already seen, Abraham and Israel would be blessed and become a great nation.

2. In chapter 1, we mentioned that God will bless and curse the nations depending on their treatment of Israel.
3. God promised to bless the world through Israel, and in this chapter, we will see how God is fulfilling that promise. We will look at a few of examples of how Israel is a blessing to the nations and how one specific government agency is helping transform some of the poorest nations. Finally, we will list some individual Jews that have profoundly affected the world in the last century.

## Israel Is Blessing the World through Food Exports

Those who come He shall cause to take root in Jacob;
Israel shall blossom and bud,
And fill the face of the world with fruit. (Isaiah 27:6)

Israel doesn't just feed its own people which is a miracle, but it has become a major exporter of fresh produce, fulfilling Isaiah's prophecy that Israel would fill the world with fruit.

Israel's exports include the following:

| Fruit | Per cent Produced | Tons/Annum |
|---|---|---|
| Citrus Fruit[1] | 33 | 160,000 |
| Dates[2] | 42 | 15,000 |
| Pomegranate[3] | 38 | 20,000 |
| Persimmon | 46 | 16,000 |
| Avocado[4] | 70 | 70,000 |
| Mangos[5] | 40 | 20,000 |
| Olive oil[6] | 6 | 1,000 |

Table 12.1 - Fresh Produce Exports

In southern Israel, eight small communities, with just 3,000 residents living on the edge of the Negev Desert, produce 150,000 tons of fresh vegetables each year, which accounts for 60 per cent of the total vegetable exports of Israel.

Scientists have created a hybrid tomato that ripens much slower than other tomatoes in hot climates. This is significant because it improves quality of the global export of fresh fruit by extending its shelf life.

That is God's blessing on Israel so she can be a blessing to the world.

## Israel Is Blessing the World in Health

Israel is a world leader in medical R&D. The list of medical breakthroughs that can be credited to Israel is large, and it is impossible to list them all here. As recently as July 2017, researchers developed a test that detects Parkinson's disease both more definitively and much earlier. Early, accurate detection improves the prognosis for millions of sufferers of this degenerative brain disease worldwide.[277] Doctors have also developed new methods for delivering insulin to millions of diabetes sufferers around the world. This new method improves their quality of life of type 1 diabetics worldwide.[278]

Jerusalem-based pharmaceutical giant TEVA has become a major producer of generic pharmaceuticals. TEVA produces 120 billion tablets annually in eighty-seven nations.[279] Generic medications are more affordable, making them more accessible worldwide. One example is TEVA's 40 mg version of Copaxone, which accounts for a staggering 68.5 per cent of total Copaxone prescriptions in the United States.[280,281]

### *Israel Is Blessing the World with Digital Technology*

Today the world's population is 7 billion, and there are 6.8 billion cell phone subscriptions. It is Israel that is leading the world in cell phone technology. Here are just three examples:

1. Currently mobile phones cannot be used in flight, but Israel companies have successfully tested in-flight cell phone use, and it is only a matter of time before people will be able to call from planes.[282]
2. Project RAY has developed the world's first smart phone for people with visual disabilities.[283]
3. Israeli start-up company StoreDot has developed a technology that can charge a mobile phone in just thirty seconds.[284]

Computers more powerful than those that guided man to the moon are in homes across the globe, and as we saw in chapter 10, Israel is leading the world in computer technology and cyber-security. These advances are not just aiding Israel but the high-tech industry around the globe.

## Israel Is Blessing the World with Security and Military Advances

Today missiles are flying into Israel on a regular basis, but it takes 445 Hamas and Hezbollah missiles for Israel to suffer one death. Is this because Arab terrorist have really bad aim, or is it because God is protecting and blessing His people?[285]

In an opinion piece for the *Jerusalem Post*, Michael Eisenstadt and David Pollock from the Washington Institute say that there has been a security shift in recent times. For years, Israel was reliant on the United States, but the balance has shifted. More than at any other time, America relies on Israel for security.[286,287] The most powerful nation on the planet is becoming more reliant on its partnership with Israel for security than ever before.

As we saw in chapter 10, Israel's advancements in military R&D and production are a fulfilment of God's promise to Abraham that Israel would bless the world. The *Jerusalem Post* in March 2017 reported that Israel's military exports for 2016 was a staggering US$6.8 billion[288], making it the tenth-largest arms exporting nation. Even more significant, the three major importers of Israeli weaponry were India (the second most populous nation), Azerbaijan (a Muslim nation that was a former Soviet state), and the United States (the world's largest exporter of military equipment).[289,290]

## MASHAV and CINADCO

*Give a man a fish, and you feed him for a day.*
*Teach a man to fish, and you feed him for a lifetime.*

—Unknown

We have already seen how Israel has transformed deserts and malaria-ridden swamp lands into a glorious oasis. Such has been the transformation that Israel has become an exporter of food. Yet, Israel does not only give poor nations *fish to eat* ; through the Agriculture Ministry, she is teaching some of the world's poorest nations *to fish*. Maybe this is Israel's greatest contribution to the betterment of life on earth.

Israel's Agency for International Development Cooperation (MASHAV) was established in 1957 by then foreign minister Golda Meir following a trip to some of Africa's most underdeveloped nations.[291] Its major affiliate, the Centre for International Agricultural Development Cooperation (CINADCO), was established in 1983 to facilitate Israel's commitment to partner with emerging nations. CINADCO's director, Yakov Poleg, made this statement in October 2016:

> Surrounded by an inhospitable mix of barren desert and malaria-ridden swampland, the fledgling State of Israel had little food with which to sustain its increasingly hungry inhabitants. Fast forward a mere six-and-a-half decades, and the Little Country that Could is not only nourishing its own eight million citizens, but is also helping developing countries around the world do the same.[292]

Since its inception, MASHAV/CINADCO has trained some 270,000 men and women from 132 nations in Israel and abroad. One of the biggest training courses is the AgroStudies apprenticeship program, which has trained about 7,000 students from twenty countries in the past eleven years. The students then return home with a wealth of new knowledge and experience.[293]

In an interview with the *Jerusalem Post* (September 5, 2016), Agriculture and Forests Minister Lyonpo Yeshey Dorji of Bhutan, a landlocked Asian country with no diplomatic relations with Israel, expressed his eagerness to further agricultural cooperation with Israel during a visit to the Jewish state. Dorji was in Israel to witness the graduation of Bhutanese students from the apprenticeship program.[294]

They have also developed many other projects worldwide.

Just as God blessed Israel turning wastelands into quality farmland, Israel now uses the knowledge she has learned to bless the world.

## India

One of Israel's greatest agricultural success stories is its partnership with India. The Indo-Israel Agriculture Project involves both MASHAV and CINADCO working with the Indian Agriculture Ministry's Mission for Integrated Development of Horticulture. Already they have established fifteen of a planned twenty-six centres of excellence. The goals of these centres are threefold: to increase Indian crop diversity, to increase crop productivity, and to make more efficient use of the available resources. To accomplish these goals, Israel focuses on sharing her expertise in water recycling. The project hopes to see all twenty-six centres fully operational by the end of 2017. The success of this partnership has led similar ventures in the Asian subcontinent, with projects in China, Vietnam, the Philippines, Myanmar, and Nepal.

## Africa: Food for the Future

Israeli joint projects are seen not only in Asia but also in some of the poorest African nations.

MASHAV and CINADCO is negotiating with *Rwanda* to replicate India's Centre of Excellence in their war and hunger-ravaged nation. When it opens, it will serve as a hub for agricultural training by adapting Israeli farming technologies to local needs. The hope is that it will increase fruit and vegetable productivity to the point where the nation will not just feed its 12 million people but provide Rwanda with an export industry.

Unlike India, the joint venture the Rwandan Centre will be fully funded by Israel.

*Ethiopia* is working MASHAV and USAID to develop projects with the country's Agriculture Ministry, focusing on avocados and mangoes.[295] This partnership has meant that Ethiopia has begun to export of avocadoes.[296]

In *Kenya*, Lake Victoria's fish stocks were being decimated because of high levels of pollution. The problem was exacerbated because, at the same time, the demand for fish around the lake was increasing. The Kenyan government signed a trilateral cooperation agreement MASHAV and the GIZ to use Israeli hi-tech methods to improve fish farming and to empower the local fishermen to restore the fish catch to previous levels.[297,298] Another program is the Galana Kulalu Food Security Project, which is using newly-developed Israeli irrigation practices to cultivate corn.[299]

*Cameroon* and Israel have signed a three-year agreement with the IFAD to send Israeli experts to academic institutions to help train farmers and young people.[300,301]

*Ghana* is collaborating with Israel and Germany to create a variety of projects and training programs.[302] The focus of these projects is citrus growing and beekeeping.

*Senegal* has entered into a partnership with Israel and Italy to introduce low-pressure drip irrigation systems to aid farmers in seventy villages.[303]

As a further sign of the growing ties between Israel and Africa, Israel has committed to several smaller projects in Malawi and Burkina Faso. For the first time, in December 2016, Israel hosted seven ministers and many other top officials from over a dozen West African countries at an agricultural conference.

Israel is sharing its breakthrough agricultural technologies with not only African and Asian nations but also South American countries.

## Individual Jews Have Great Influence

Not only has the nation of Israel blessed and impacted the world, but individual Jews from around the world have influenced the world and in many cases changed the way we think. A staggering statistic is that since 1901, one-quarter of 1 per cent of the world's population has been awarded almost a quarter of all Nobel prizes given. In this century, there has been a total of fifty Jewish recipients of Nobel prizes.[304] The table below shows the various fields where Jews have excelled and been recognised and named Nobel laureates.

| NUMBER | FIELD |
|---|---|
| 35 | Chemistry |
| 53 | Medicine |
| 52 | Physics |
| 15 | Literature |
| 28 | Economics |
| 9 | Peace |

Table 12.2 - Number of Jewish Nobel Prize Winners[305]

One of the world's most outspoken atheists, Richard Dawkins, acknowledges, somewhat begrudgingly, that he cannot explain why Jews, with a worldwide population of just 13.9 million, have such a disproportionate number of Nobel laureates. He commented, "I haven't thought it through. I don't know. But I don't think it is a minor thing; it is colossal."[306]

In addition to Nobel prizes, Jews also have dominated lesser-known awards, receiving 25 per cent of the Kyoto Prizes, 34 per cent of the Wolf Foundation Prizes, 38 per cent of the US National Medal of Science and 53 per cent of the Grande Médaille of the French Academy of Sciences. [307,308,309,310]

### Science

From the table above, we can see that Jewsish scientists have dominated the Nobel Prizes. That dominance is evident in that three of the top ten most influential scientists of the twentieth century were Jews.[311] Although lists are often subjective, all rank Einstein, Freud, and Bohr in the top ten

*Albert Einstein* was a German-born theoretical physicist who is consistently named the most influential scientist of the twentieth century. In 1999, *Time* magazine described Einstein as the "pre-eminent scientist in a century dominated by science" when they named him the Person of the Century.[312]

Einstein developed the theory of relativity and gave the world the most famous equation of the twentieth century: $E = mc^2$. He received the 1921 Nobel Prize in Physics for his services to theoretical physics, especially for his discovery of the law of the photoelectric effect.[313] Einstein published more than 300 scientific works and more than 150 non-scientific works.

*Sigmund Freud*, Austrian neurologist and physiologist and father of psychoanalysis, was recognised as one of the most influential and authoritative thinkers of the century.[314] He was the co-founder of the psychoanalytic school of psychology.

*Niels Henrik David Bohr*, a Danish physicist, redefined how the world understood atomic structure and quantum mechanics and received the Nobel Prize in Physics in 1922.[315] Bohr worked alongside many of the top physicists on the Manhattan Project.[316]

In another survey, *Julius Robert Oppenheimer*, an American theoretical physicist, was ranked the eighty-seventh most influential scientist of all time.[317] Professor of physics at the University of California, Berkeley, Oppenheimer became known as the "father of the atomic bomb" for his leadership role in the Manhattan Project.

## *Economics*

Jews have been awarded twenty-eight Nobel Prizes for Economics. Until recently, two of the most influential world economic chairs were Jews. Although he did not win a Nobel Prize, Ben Bernanke, a Jew from Augusta, Georgia, held the most powerful economic position in the world as Chairman of the US Federal Reserve from 2006 to 2014. Like Bernanke, Dominique Strauss-Kahn is not a Nobel laureate, but from 2007 to 2011 he was the head of the International Monetary Fund.

In March 2016, the Jewish Telegraphic Agency (JTA) reported that eleven of the fifty wealthiest people on the planet were Jews.[318] This again shows that Israel is blessed and favoured by God, as He remembers His covenant with Israel.

*Diplomacy*

Jewish influence in the world is not limited to science and economics. Henry Kissinger was a Jew born in Furth, Germany, who moved to America in 1938 to flee the impending Holocaust. He became one of the most influential diplomats of the twentieth century. He served as the US National Security Advisor from 1969 to 1973 and Secretary of State from 1973 to 1977. He was the most influential secretary of state in the last fifty years. His diplomatic skills opened up the opportunity for Richard Nixon's groundbreaking visits to Beijing and Moscow in 1972.[319,320] He won the Nobel Peace Prize after negotiating the ceasefire agreements that ended US involvement in the Vietnam War. He was instrumental in brokering a peace treaty between Israel and Egypt in 1979, which has remained intact to this day.

He remains a controversial figure, but even after his term, his advice has been sought by world leaders, including US presidents.

## Conclusion

How can we explain 0.23 per cent of the world's population exerting such significant influence on the world's science, diplomacy, and the economy? Can what Dawkins saw as significant but unexplainable be explained? No one can ever make sense of the miracle that is Israel if they do not believe in God. In an interview with CBS TV on October 5, 1956, then Israeli prime minister David Ben Gurion uttered this famous quote: "In Israel, in order to be a realist, you must believe in miracles."[321]

Israel is at the forefront of research and development, and by sharing those breakthroughs with the world, she is fulfilling God's promise to bless the world through Israel. Israel has grown to be a powerful, influential player on the world stage, but the best is yet to come. I believe the greatest promise given to Israel is yet to be fulfilled. That is the theme of the last chapter, in which we look at Israel's glorious future.

# CHAPTER 13

## Romans—Israel's Glorious Future

*I had faith in Israel before it was established. I have in it now. I believe it has a glorious future before it.*

—Harry S. Truman

So far, we have looked at the rebirth of the state of Israel and how it has grown into an international powerhouse. We have also examined why God chose to bless Israel.

My purpose was not to write an apologetic showing how the Jews "missed it" regarding the Messiah; it was to show Israel was, is, and will always be God's covenant people. The book shows God continues to bless and favour Israel because of the covenant and illustrates that one of the great Old testament prophecies, Ezekiel's vision of the valley of dry bones, is being fulfilled in our lifetime.

In this final chapter, we will look at Israel's future and how one promise remains unfulfilled. Ezekiel saw the day when the nation would accept Yeshua, Jesus, as their Messiah. God, who would then breathe His Holy Spirit into the nation, leading Israel to become an exceedingly great *spiritual* army.

> Also He said to me, "Prophesy to the breath, prophesy, son of man, and say to the breath, 'Thus says the Lord God: "Come from the four winds, O breath, and breathe on these slain, that they may live."'" So I prophesied as He commanded me, and breath came into them, and they lived, and stood upon their feet, an exceedingly great army. (Ezekiel 37:9–10)

Israel's future is far more glorious than all that has gone before, and what will happen will shock the world. At this point in history, Israel as a nation still rejects their Messiah but a day is coming when they will embrace Him. He will then return is establish God's everlasting Kingdom in the New Jerusalem.[322]

### Down but Not Out

Our journey begins with Paul's description of Israel's current state as a nation that has stumbled.

> I say then, have they stumbled that they should fall? Certainly not! But through their fall, to provoke them to jealousy, salvation has come to the Gentiles. (Romans 11:11)

The Jews have stumbled over the person the Bible calls a stumbling stone, a cornerstone, and a rock of offense, their Messiah.[323,324,325]

The good news is that the stumble is not fatal! God has not condemned and replaced them.[326] Paul uses two totally different Greek words that both translate to "fall." It could be read, "I say then, have they stumbled that they should *be condemned?* Certainly not! But through their *slip up*, to provoke them to jealousy, salvation has come to the Gentiles." [327,328,329]

God is using Israel's slip up to provoke the nation to jealousy. They can see the Gentiles, who had no desire to be right with God, now right with Him through their Messiah. The Jews, on the other hand, have sought to be right with God but have never succeeded, because they are unable to keep the Law of Moses.[330]

There is coming a day when the nation will recognise the Messiah, and that will be the day when Ezekiel's prophecy is fulfilled in its entirety. They will live, stand, and be an exceedingly great army. Again, Paul says,

> Now if their fall is riches for the world, and their failure riches for the Gentiles, how much more their fullness! For I speak to you Gentiles; inasmuch as I am an apostle to the Gentiles, I magnify my ministry, if by any means I may provoke to jealousy those who are my flesh and save some of them. For if their being cast away is the reconciling of the world, what will their acceptance be but life from the dead? (Romans 11:12–15)

All the Christian revivals and outpourings that have peppered the church age will pale in comparison to what will happen in Israel. Paul describes the revivals amongst Gentiles as reconciliation but the coming revival in Israel as life from death.

## Sight for the Blind

Paul describes Israel's current spiritual plight as a mystery that can be understood only through divine revelation, the removal of a spiritual blindness that has come upon the nation.

> For I do not desire, brethren, that you should be ignorant of this mystery, lest you should be wise in your own opinion, that blindness in part has happened to Israel until the fullness of the Gentiles has come in. And so all Israel will be saved, as it is written, "The Deliverer will come out of Zion, and He will turn away ungodliness from Jacob for this is My covenant with them,

when I take away their sins." (Romans 11:25–27)

Paul makes the bold assertion that the spiritual blindness will be lifted when the *fullness of the Gentiles* comes in. When that happens, *all* Israel will be saved. He is not saying every person that is a natural descendant from Abraham is going to be saved. In Romans 9, Paul spoke of *an Israel within Israel*, a remnant.[331] It is the remnant of Israel, the *spiritual Israel*, that will see Jesus and be saved.[332]

## The Veil Will Soon Be Lifted and Israel See Her Messiah

We know when the national revival in Israel will happen. Zechariah, 2,500 years ago, gave Israel a wonderful prophetic word foretelling Israel's national revival.

> "And I will pour on the house of David and on the inhabitants of Jerusalem the Spirit of grace and supplication; then they will look on Me whom they pierced. Yes, they will mourn for Him as one mourns for his only son, and grieve for Him as one grieves for a firstborn. (Zechariah 12:10)

This verse changed my thinking about Israel. God is going to pour out the spirit of grace and supplication on the house of David and *on the inhabitants of Jerusalem*. The only plausible interpretation is that the Jews need to be living in *an undivided* Jerusalem when God pours out the spirit. The problem was that the Jews were driven from Jerusalem 2,000 years ago, and Jesus made it clear why.

> "If you had known, even you, especially in this your day, the things that make for your peace! But now they are hidden from your eyes. For days will come upon you when your enemies will build an embankment around you, surround you and close you in on every side, and level you, and your children within you, to the ground; and they will not leave in you one stone upon another, because you did not know the time of your visitation." (Luke 19:41–44)

Many Godly men have seen the great miracle of modern Israel unfold before their eyes yet fail to see God's hand. Like Israel, who cannot see their Messiah because a veil is blinding them, many believers are blind to what God is doing in Israel. I was one. My thinking was that God drove the Jews from the land and Jerusalem because of unbelief, so before God would ever consider bringing the Jews home, they would need to have repented and accepted their Messiah. I failed to see what scripture clearly reveals that the Israelites will return from exile still in unbelief. It was this revelation of God's plan and purpose, revealed in Zechariah, that changed my thinking and attitude towards Israel.

It also explains the spirit behind all that has happened in the state of Israel, the opposition, wars, and vitriol over the last seventy years. The devil knows his time is fast running out, and when the Jews in Jerusalem accept their Messiah, his time will have run out. He is doing everything he can to stop Jews living peacefully in an undivided Jerusalem to delay this outpouring of grace and supplication.

Jerusalem is currently divided into four sections: Jewish, Muslim, Christian, and Armenian. So why am I dogmatic that Zechariah 12:10 is speaking of the Israelis and not Christians, Muslims, or Armenians? The Apostle Peter says twice in Acts that it was the Jews that crucified Jesus.[333] This same nation will be living in Jerusalem and will look on *Me whom they pierced*. It is not my purpose to perpetuate the anti-Semitic idea of deicide, which I showed in chapter 4 is nothing but a poor excuse to justify hatred of Jews. Scripture shows that Jesus' crucifixion was the predetermined plan of God.[334] It wasn't Muslims or Christians that pierced Jesus, because neither of those religious groups existed when Jesus went to the cross.[335]

When Jews are living in the undivided city of Jerusalem, God will remove the veil that has blinded them for 2,000 years, and they will know that the One their ancestors rejected and pierced is their Messiah and they will mourn for what happened.

## Two into One Doesn't Go

Many Jewish rabbis believe in two Messiahs, Messiah Ben Joseph and Messiah Ben David.[336] They believe that Messiah Ben Joseph will come only to be killed in a war against evil, sometime later, Messiah Ben David will come as the conquering king. Those rabbis believe that Zechariah is a reference to Messiah Ben Joseph and the nation is mourning His death in the battle against evil. When that happens, the stage will be set for the appearance of Messiah [Ben David].[337]

However, there are not two Messiahs each appearing once. There is one Messiah who appears twice. The Messiah's first appearance was as the suffering servant, described in detail in Isaiah 53. He was killed in the ultimate battle against evil but defeated evil by the power of the resurrection. His second appearance comes at the end of the age as the "Lion of the Tribe of Judah but cannot occur until Zechariah 12:10 is fulfilled."[338]

## Jesus, the Alpha and Omega (Aleph-Tav)

Spread throughout the Tanach are two Hebrew letters that do not form a word and remain untranslatable, *aleph* and *tav*.[339] These two Hebrew letters are the first and the last letters of the Hebrew alphabet and are literally read as *aleph-tav*.[340]

The first occurrence of *aleph-tav* is in Genesis 1:1: "In the beginning God, *aleph-tav*, created the heavens and the earth." Many scholars believe this is a hidden code within the Old Testament pointing to Yeshua, who in the Greek New Testament is called the Alpha and Omega.[341] The Apostle John tells us that Jesus is the creator.[342]

*Aleph-tav* is also found here in Zechariah 12:10:

> And I will pour on the house of David and on the inhabitants of Jerusalem the Spirit of grace and supplication; then they will behold *aleph-tav*, whom they pierced.

The Hebrew word, translated "behold" in our English Bibles, simply means to look with favour upon. Literally what is meant is that the Jews will look with favour on aleph-tav.

The same two characters appear in the Isaiah 53:6.

> All we like sheep have gone astray; we have turned, everyone, to his own way; and the Lord has laid on aleph-tav the iniquity of us all.

It is my firm belief that *aleph-tav* is a reference to Jesus.

## The New Covenant

Once Israel acknowledges that their Messiah has come, another significant prophecy will be fulfilled: the promise of a new covenant. When I say it fulfils the promise of a new covenant, I am saying Israel as a nation will embrace the New Covenant established 2,000 years ago, when their Messiah was crucified on the cross.[343]

### *The Three Covenants*

To understand Israel is to understand three covenants. The Abrahamic Covenant has the two unconditional promises: (1) Abraham would father a great nation and (2) the nation would possess its own land.[344] Two other covenants also play an important role in Israel's life. The Mosaic Covenant, unlike the first covenant, is conditional. If Israel were faithful to the commandments they would be blessed with abundance and protection, but if they rebelled, curses would come upon the people.[345] If they failed to change, the ultimate curse would be exile from the land.

> "Then the Lord will scatter you among all peoples, from one end of the earth to the other, and there you shall serve other gods, which neither you nor your fathers have known—wood and stone. And among those nations you shall find no rest, nor shall the sole of your foot have a resting place; but there the Lord will give you a trembling heart, failing eyes, and anguish of soul. (Deuteronomy 28:64–65)

The Mosaic covenant was not only conditional; it was always intended to be temporal. The Apostle Paul, a Jewish rabbi, made that point when he said Christ is the end of the law for righteousness to everyone who believes.[346] Hundreds of years earlier, Jeremiah also said a new covenant would supersede the Law.[347]

> Behold, the days are coming, says the Lord, when I will make a new covenant with the house of Israel and with the house of Judah—not according to the covenant that I made with their fathers in the day that I took them by the hand to lead them out of the land of Egypt, My covenant which they broke, though I was a husband to them, says the Lord. (Jeremiah 31:31–32)

When the New Testament uses the phrase "new covenant," it refers to the prophecy of Jeremiah 31.[348] The reason for a new covenant is that Israel could not keep the Law. If it were possible, there would have been no need for a new covenant. God says He is going to do for Israel what they could not do for themselves.

> "[T]his is the covenant that I will make with the house of Israel after those days, says the Lord: I will put My law in their minds, and write it on their hearts; and I will be their God, and they shall be My people. No more shall every man teach his neighbour, and every man his brother, saying, 'Know the Lord,' for they all shall know Me, from the least of them to the greatest of them, says the Lord. For I will forgive their iniquity, and their sin I will remember no more." (Jeremiah 31:33–34)

Ezekiel tells us when this would take place. He says that after God brings the exiles home, He will cleanse the nation from unrighteousness.

> For I will take you from among the nations, gather you out of all countries, and bring you into your own land. Then I will sprinkle clean water on you, and you shall be clean; I will cleanse you from all your filthiness and from all your idols. I will give you a new heart and put a new spirit within you; I will take the heart of stone out of your flesh and give you a heart of flesh. I will put My Spirit within you and cause you to walk in My statutes, and you will keep My judgments and do them. (Ezekiel 36:24–27)

## The Devil's Last Gasp

The central theme throughout this work has been the unconditional and everlasting covenant that God cut with Abraham. The covenant concerned a people, the descendants of Abraham, Isaac, and Jacob. It was also about a land, the Promised Land. We have looked at the unfolding miracle that is modern-day Israel and what is to come for the apple of God's eye. We have seen how the world seeks to divide the land of Israel and that Israel's Muslim neighbours have made no secret of their desire to destroy her. Despite the institutionalised hatred of nations and bodies such as the United Nations, we have seen how Israel has thrived and grown into an international powerhouse.

Our journey ends sometime soon. The devil will make one last effort to thwart God's plan. But just as before, when he thinks he has won, disaster strikes him. This time it will be fatal when Jesus returns and establishes His Kingdom in Jerusalem.

> Behold, the day of the Lord is coming,
> And your spoil will be divided in your midst.
> For I will gather all the nations to battle against Jerusalem;
> The city shall be taken,
> The houses rifled,
> And the women ravished.
> Half of the city shall go into captivity,
> But the remnant of the people shall not be cut off from the city.

> Then the Lord will go forth
> And fight against those nations,
> As He fights in the day of battle.
> And in that day His feet will stand on the Mount of Olives,
> Which faces Jerusalem on the east.
> And the Mount of Olives shall be split in two,
> From east to west,
> Making a very large valley;
> Half of the mountain shall move toward the north
> And half of it toward the south. (Zechariah 14:1–4)

Zechariah reveals that God will allow the devil to gather the nations in Jerusalem and it will fall. It's not the purpose here to speculate as to the identity of these nations except to say the most poisonous anti-Semitic nations today are Muslim nations whose leaders make no secret of their desire to see Israel annihilated. An example of the hate-filled rhetoric that spews from the mouths of Islamist leaders was posted on Twitter by Iran's Supreme Leader Ayatollah Ali Khamenei. He tweeted, "This barbaric, wolflike & infanticidal regime of Israel which spares no crime has no cure but to be annihilated."[349] He left nothing to the imagination, publicly declaring that the only cure to the Israel problem is her annihilation.

Another Iranian leader, Ali Shirazi, made comments that were no less abhorrent: "The Zionist regime will soon be destroyed, and this generation will be witness to its destruction."[350,351]

Influential Iranian Imam, Ayatollah Mohammed Ali Movahedi-Kermani, said, "The issue of Palestine is an Islamic issue. The Islamic world must come together to destroy the false Israeli regime … If this happens, nothing will be left of Israel."[352]

This is an official statement from the Iranian Ministry of Defence:

> "If once the destruction and demise of occupying Israel was an impossible and unattainable dream, today thanks to the historic and intelligent actions of Imam Khomeini, it has become possible and is actually in the process of occurring."[353]

We have already seen that these views are not limited to Iran. Most Muslim nations in the Middle East have made similar threats for more than seventy years. They are rooted in the words of their Prophet Muhammad, who linked the age to the demise of Israel.

> *The last hour would not come unless the Muslims will fight against the Jews* and the Muslims

would kill them until the Jews would hide themselves behind a stone or a tree and a stone or a tree would say: Muslim, or the servant of Allah, there is a Jew behind me; come and kill him.[354]

## Maranatha—Come, Lord Jesus

Just prior to Jesus' return, anti-Semitism and hatred of the Jews will reach a crescendo. Nations that I believe to be Muslim will invade Jerusalem. Jeremiah gives a grave warning of what these times will be like:

> Ah, that day is awesome;
> There is none like it!
> It is a time of trouble for Jacob,
> But he shall be delivered from it. (Jeremiah 30:7 TANACH)

What Jeremiah called a time of trouble for Jacob (Israel), Jesus called *The Great Tribulation*. Both warned that it would be so devastating that without God's intervention, no Jew would survive.[355] Jeremiah and Jesus assure us that God has promised to intervene on behalf of Israel.

There is a wonderful word that only appears once in the scriptures—Maranatha.[356] It is a compound word and has proved difficult to accurately translate. Some scholars believe the two words are *maranâ* and *thâ'*, which would translate as, "Our Lord come," while others believe the words are *maran* and *'athâ'*, which would mean, "The Lord has come." What a powerful word. It could be a prayer and a cry for help, "Our Lord come!" But it could also be a declaration of faith: "Our Lord has come!" Jesus has both come and is coming.

This brings us to the last piece in the puzzle. When will God intervene to end the brutality of the invading armies and liberate Jerusalem and the state of Israel forever?

Jeremiah made it clear that God will intervene to save the "Apple of His Eye," and Zechariah says he will return to the Mount of Olives just outside of Jerusalem's city wall.

> His feet will stand on the Mount of Olives,
> Which faces Jerusalem on the east.
> And the Mount of Olives shall be split in two,
> From east to west,
> Making a very large valley;
> Half of the mountain shall move toward the north
> And half of it toward the south. (Zechariah 14:4)

When will Jesus return and fulfil Jeremiah and Zechariah's prophecies? The answer was given 2,000 years ago by Jesus and shows why the devil is so determined to drive the Jews out of Jerusalem. We have already seen, Jesus prophesied that the land would be invaded because their descendants failed to recognise their Messiah. But He also pointed to a time when they would acknowledge Him as their Messiah.

> "See! Your house is left to you desolate; and assuredly, I say to you, *you shall not see Me until the time comes when you say, 'Blessed is He who comes in the name of the Lord!'*" (Matthew 23:39, emphasis mine)

Jesus entered Jerusalem a week before His crucifixion to the cries of, "Hosanna to the Son of David! Blessed is He who comes in the name of the Lord!"[357] Just a few days later, the religious leaders stirred up the same people to cry out, "Crucify Him!"[358]

Jesus is now waiting for the Jewish spiritual leaders to finally recognise Him as Messiah and say, *"Baruch ha-ba b'shem Adonai"* and with that invitation, these prophecies will be fulfilled in a day.[359]

## Conclusion

The Old Testament prophets, together with Jesus, show a clear progression that started over one hundred years ago, with the first *Aliyah*. When the Jews live in an undivided Jerusalem, God will pour out His Spirit ushering in a mighty end-times revival. The devil, who knows his time is up, will make one last effort to destroy the "Apple of God's eye" and in the midst of horrendous tribulation the nation will cry out *baruch ha-ba b'shem Adonai*. With that invitation, Yeshua will return to the Mount of Olives just outside the city wall and His kingdom will be established in Jerusalem.

### Baruch ha-ba b'shem Adonai

(Footnotes)

1 http://www.israelagri.com/?CategoryID=522&ArticleID=1158&SearchParam=olive+oil+export.
2 http://www.israelagri.com/?CategoryID=522&ArticleID=1121&SearchParam=export.
3 http://www.israelagri.com/?CategoryID=522&ArticleID=1034&SearchParam=export.
4 http://www.israelagri.com/?CategoryID=522&ArticleID=1036&SearchParam=export.
5 http://www.israelagri.com/?CategoryID=522&ArticleID=1035&SearchParam=export.
6 www.israel21c.org/israeli-olive-oil-comes-of-age/.

# ENDNOTES

1 Iran's president from 2005 to 2013.
2 Turkey's president
3 NIS: The New Israeli Sheckle is Israel's currency, valued at roughly 1/3 of a US dollar.
4 http://www.jpost.com/Opinion/Israels-achievements-on-its-68th-birthday-453656.
5 http://www.jewishvirtuallibrary.org/jsource/Quote/TwainJews.htm.
6 https://www.brainyquote.com/quotes/quotes/d/davidbeng146266.html.
7 Yeshua the Hebrew name that corresponds to the Greek Iēsous, translated Jesus or Joshua.
8 See Zechariah 12:10.
9 See Romans 11:17.
10 See 2 Corinthians 3:14.
11 Epistle to the Magnesians, sourced from http://www.yashanet.com/library/fathers.htm.
12 Ibid.
13 One of the "greatest" of church fathers, he was known as "the Golden Mouthed." He was a missionary preacher famous for his sermons and addresses. *The Roots of Christian Anti-Semitism* by Malcolm Hay.
14 https://en.wikipedia.org/wiki/Martin_Luther_and_antisemitism.
15 See John 4:22.
16 See chapters 13 and 14.
17 See Romans 11:15.
18 See chapter 18 for a fuller explanation.
19 See Exodus 19:5 and Deuteronomy 14:2.
20 See Zechariah 2:8.
21 See Genesis 15.
22 https://www.talkjesus.com/threads/covenant.56134/
23 See Genesis 12:3.
24 http://www.jpost.com/Israel-News/Politics-And-Diplomacy/Watch-Israel-trash-UNESCOs-Jerusalem-resolution-470917.
25 See Jeremiah 31.
26 Pogroms are the organised massacre of Jews in Russia or Eastern Europe.
27 Judensau (German for "Jews' sow" or "Jewish sow"), also known as Saujuden, is a folk-art depiction of Jews in obscene contact with a large female pig, dating back to the thirteenth century.
28 Bible translators translate Cush, Etheopia but is more Sudan.
29 Jonathan Edwards, *The Works of Jonathan Edwards*, vol. 1 (Banner of Truth, 1976), 607.
30 From first volume of Sermons, 1855, as cited in Iain Murray, *The Puritan Hope*, 256.
31 George Ladd, "Historic Premillennialism," in *The Meaning of the Millennium: Four Views*, ed. Robert G. Clouse (Downers Grove, IL: InterVarsity, 1977), 28.
32 Jürgen Moltmann, *The Way of Jesus Christ: Christology in Messianic Dimensions*. Trans. Margaret Kohl

(San Francisco: Harper San Francisco, 1990), 35.
33 http://www.theologicalstudies.org/resource-library/supersessionism/327-12-reasons-why-supersessionism-replacement-theology-is-not-a-biblical-doctrine.
34 http://www.sixdaywar.org/content/threats.asp.
35 Ibid.
36 https://chnm.gmu.edu/revolution/d/284/.
37 http://www.jpost.com/Opinion/Berlin-Jerusalem-and-dual-loyalty-413130.
38 http://www.goodreads.com/quotes/320253-who-has-inflicted-this-upon-us-who-has-made-us.
39 http://www.ynetnews.com/articles/0,7340,L-4663579,00.html.
40 Ezekiel 37:11.
41 In the second century CE, the Romans crushed the revolt of Shimon Bar Kokhba (132 CE), during which Jerusalem and Judea were regained and the area of Judea was renamed Palaestina in an attempt to minimize Jewish identification with the land of Israel.
42 Eretz Yisrael is the traditional Hebrew and Yiddish name for "The Land of Israel."
43 Aliyah is the immigration of Jews from the all over the world to the Land of Israel.
44 A caliphate is an area containing an Islamic steward, a person considered a religious successor to the Islamic prophet Muhammad and a leader of the entire Muslim community.
45 http://www.mythsandfacts.org/conflict/mandate_for_palestine/mandate_for_palestine.htm.
46 Winston Churchill was the Secretary of State for the Colonies from 13 February, 1921 - 19 October, 1922
47 https://en.wikipedia.org/wiki/Churchill_White_Paper.
48 In 1915 Sir Henry McMahon, British High Commissioner in Egypt, offered Sherif Hussein of Mecca an independent Arab state if he would help the British fight against the Ottoman Turks.
49 Allan Gerson, *Israel, The West Bank, and International Law* (London: Taylor and Francis, 2012), 44.
50 http://avalon.law.yale.edu/20th_century/palmanda.asp.
51 Ibid.
52 http://azure.org.il/include/print.php?id=319.
53 http://www.meforum.org/2464/quran-covenant-with-jewish-people.
54 https://en.wikipedia.org/wiki/Muslim_supporters_of_Israel#cite_note-87.
55 Verse 21 of Surat Al-Maeda of the Holy Quran.
56 https://en.wikipedia.org/wiki/Muslim_supporters_of_Israel#Kuwait.
57 https://palestineisraelconflict.wordpress.com/2013/10/26/a-muslim-cleric-there-was-never-a-palestinian-people/.
58 http://quran.com/5/20-21
59 http://quran.com/17/104
60 http://www.memritv.org/clip_transcript/en/3389.htm
61 The Palestine Liberation Organization (PLO) was created in 1964 in Cairo. The PLO's originally-stated goal was the "liberation of Palestine" through armed struggle while seeking to destroy the existence of Zionism in the Middle East.
62 A *moshava* is a form of rural Jewish settlement in the Ottoman period.

63 Michael Rydelnik, *Understanding the Arab-Israeli Conflict* (Chicaga: Moody Press, 2007), 169.
64 Ibid.
65 Peel Commission report 1937.
66 Ibid.
67 https://www.unwatch.org/un-to-adopt-20-resolutions-against-israel-3-on-rest-of-the-world/.
68 https://www.forbes.com/2010/06/23/israel-hamas-middle-east-opinions-columnists-daniel-freedman.html.
69 Ibid.
70 https://www.unwatch.org/un-to-adopt-20-resolutions-against-israel-3-on-rest-of-the-world/
71 Ibid.
72 https://www.knesset.gov.il/docs/eng/megilat_eng.htm.
73 Ibid.
74 Reported in the *New York Times* on May 15, 1948. http://www.meforum.org/3082/azzam-genocide-threat.
75 http://www.sixdaywar.co.uk/crucial_quotes.htm.
76 Ibid.
77 Ibid.
78 British Prime Minister Harold Wilson (1964–1970, 1974–1976). *The Times*, June 1, 1967.
79 http://azure.org.il/include/print.php?id=319.
80 http://www.haaretz.com/news/hamas-official-we-must-lay-foundation-for-a-tomorrow-without-zionists-1.267484.
81 https://www.buzzfeed.com/jerusalemcenter/sworn-to-destruction-20-threats-iranian-leaders-m-hys5.
82 http://www.adl.org/israel-international/israel-middle-east/content/AG/inaccuracies-Israel-disinterest-peace-compromises.html?referrer=https://www.google.com.au/#.VzWr15F97IV.
83 Judge Sir Elihu Lauterpacht, *Jerusalem and the Holy Places* (London: The Anglo-Israel Association, 1968). http://mythsandfacts.org/article_view.asp?articleID=237
84 http://www.jewishvirtuallibrary.org/population-of-israel-1948-present.
85 *Aliyah* is the immigration of Jews from the all over the world to the Land of Israel.
86 http://mfa.gov.il/MFA/PressRoom/2010/Pages/Address_PM_Netanyahu_at_Auschwitz_27-Jan-2010.aspx.
87 See previous chapter.
88 Final Solution is the term adopted by the Nazis for its plan to exterminate the Jewish people.
89 http://www.haaretz.com/israel-news/1.681525.
90 https://www.ushmm.org/wlc/en/article.php?ModuleId=10005459.
91 http://www.jewishvirtuallibrary.org/report-on-the-acquiescence-of-fdr-government-in-the-murder-of-the-jews-january-1944.
92 http://www.pbs.org/jewishamericans/jewish_life/anti-semitism.html.
93 https://www.gilderlehrman.org/history-by-era/world-war-ii/resources/immigration-policy-world-war-ii.
94 https://qz.com/553393/a-survey-of-americans-on-jewish-refugees-in-the-1930s-shows-history-is-repeating-itself/.
95 http://www.jewishvirtuallibrary.org/jsource/Holocaust/treasrep.html.

96 Ibid

97 Ibid.

98 See chapter 2.

99 See Ezekiel 37:11.

100 Israel was divided in 930BCE while Ezekiel was a prophet during the Babylonian captivity between 593 and 571BCE.

101 The divided nation is known by various titles. Judah is also known as the "Southern Kingdom." The other ten tribes are known as the "Northern Kingdom," Israel and Ephraim.

102 Theodor Herzl was an Austrian/Hungarian journalist, playwright, political activist, and writer. He was called the father of modern Zionism.

103 For example, see Ezekiel 37:11, Isaiah 11:11–12, Jeremiah 30:3, Hosea 3:4–5.

104 The name Jew is derived from the Hebrew word Yehudi, meaning "from the Tribe of Judah" or "from the Kingdom of Judah." When we speak of the Jews, we are strictly speaking only of the Hebrews that are descended from the "Southern Kingdom," Judah, Jacob's forth son, and Benjamin, his twelfth.

105 Jeroboam, the son of Nebat, was the leader of the rebellion that split the kingdom. See 1 Kings 12.

106 For example, see 2 Kings 13:2 and 11; 14:24; and 15:9, 18, 24, and 28.

107 See 2 Samuel 7:16.

108 https://askdrbrown.org/library/what-are-ten-lost-tribes-israel.

109 Ibid.

110 Ibid.

111 Ibid.

112 Rehoboam, who led the rebellion against Judah, was an Ephraimite, and so the ten tribes are often referred to as "Ephraim."

113 http://www.pbs.org/wgbh/nova/israel/losttribes.html.

114 Ibid.

115 Jewish Voice Ministries mission is to proclaim the Gospel, engage the church concerning Israel and the Jewish people, and grow the Messianic Jewish Community.

116 The International Christian Embassy was founded in 1980 by evangelical Christians to express their support for the State of Israel and the Jewish people.

117 Y chromosome in humans is a sex chromosome found only in male cells.

118 Levites were the priests and were spread throughout the nation. Every community would have Levite priests.

119 Kohanim served as priests in ancient Judaism, and present-day Kohanim are accorded special status in Orthodox Judaism.

120 A genetic marker is a gene or DNA sequence that can be used to identify individuals or species.

121 http://www.pbs.org/wgbh/nova/israel/familycohanim.html.

122 Ibid.

123 Bene is the plural of the Hebrew word Ben, which means "son of." Bene Israel translates to "Sons of Israel."

124 See Deuteronomy 6:4.

125 Saniwar is the Hindi word for Saturday. Teli is a caste traditionally occupied in the pressing of oil in India.

126 Hannakuh was a feast to commemorate the dedication of the 2$^{nd}$ temple and was first celebrated when the miracle of the oil occurred in 138 BCE after bene Israel arrived on Indian shores.
127 http://www.jewishpress.com/sections/magazine/glimpses-ajh/the-american-indian-descended-from-the-ten-lost-tribes-part-ii/2015/02/04/.
128 Sons of Manasseh.
129 http://www.jpost.com/Opinion/Columnists/Homecoming-for-a-Lost-Tribe-of-Israel
130 Lost Jewish tribe "found in Zimbabwe" *BBC News Monday*, March 8, 2010. http://news.bbc.co.uk/2/hi/8550614.stm.
131 David Goldstein is an American human geneticist. He trained in theoretical population genetics at Stanford University.
132 http://www.pbs.org/wgbh/nova/israel/familylemba.html.
133 Several wars were fought between the divided kingdoms of Judah and Israel.
134 *Kashrut* is the body of Jewish religious laws concerning the suitability of food and the use of ritual objects. It comes from the Hebrew root as the more commonly known word *kosher*.
135 The chief rabbinate of Israel is the supreme rabbinic and spiritual authority for Judaism in Israel.
136 The Law of Return is Israeli legislation, passed on July 5, 1950, which gives Jews the right to live in Israel and to gain Israeli citizenship.
137 http://www.theguardian.com/world/2010/jan/17/israel-lost-tribes-pashtun.
138 Ibid.
139 Telugu is a language native to India.
140 The oral traditions of the Jews. Bene Ephraim call them Cavilah traditions.
141 Bar mitzvah is the Jewish coming-of-age ritual.
142 A *chuppah* is the canopy under which a Jewish couple stands during their wedding ceremony.
143 See Zechariah 2:8.
144 See Jeremiah 31:31–34, Ezekiel 37:14.
145 See Deuteronomy 28.
146 See Deuteronomy 28:64–68.
147 See Zechariah 9:11.
148 See chapter 3.
149 David Ben Gurion's speech to the Twenty-first Zionist Congress, Basel, 1937. http://www.ahavat-israel.com/eretz/peace.php.
150 To see the proposed borders, see figure 3.
151 See the armistice borders in figure 4.
152 See chapter 5 and the statement from Palazzi.
153 On October 29, 1956, Israeli armed forces pushed into Egypt toward the Suez Canal after Egyptian president Gamal Abdel Nasser nationalized the canal in July. The conflict ended on November 7, 1956, and the Israeli, British, and French troops in late 1956 and early 1957 were replaced with International UN force.
154 Suing for peace is an act by a warring nation to initiate a peace process. Suing for peace is usually initiated by the losing party in an attempt to stave off an unconditional surrender.
155 The Palestine Liberation Organization (PLO) was created in 1964 in Cairo. The PLO's originally-stated

goal was the "liberation of Palestine" through armed struggle while seeking to destroy the existence of Zionism in the Middle East.

156 The Palestinian Centre for Public Opinion is a research institute in "Palestine" and conducts national and regional field surveys, studies, and research.

157 Founded in 2003, The Israel Project (TIP) is a non-partisan American educational organization dedicated to informing the media and public conversation about Israel and the Middle East.

158 http://www.jpost.com/Diplomacy-and-Politics/6-in-10-Palestinians-reject-2-state-solution-survey-finds.

159 . The Oslo Peace Accord is a plan that was to outline the necessary elements and conditions for a future Palestinian state "on the basis of the United nations Security Council Resolutions 242 and 338."

160 http://www.nybooks.com/articles/2013/08/15/what-future-israel/.

161 http://www.jpost.com/Middle-East/Hamas-says-it-would-never-accept-two-state-solution-wont-give-up-one-inch-of-land-339682.

162 http://www.jewishvirtuallibrary.org/jsource/Terrorism/Hamas_covenant_complete.html

163 Ibid.

164 Ibid.

165 http://israelipalestinian.procon.org/view.answers.php?questionID=001327.

166 Ibid.

167 http://www.nytimes.com/2016/02/10/opinion/the-many-mideast-solutions.html?_r=0.

168 Ibid.

169 http://www.gatestoneinstitute.org/4151/palestinians-recognition-israel-jewish-state.

170 Ibid.

171 See Jeremiah 29:11

172 This is from the Tree of Live Version.

173 A High Place, (Hebrew bamot or bamah) was a raised altar or hilltop shrine in ancient Israel.

174 See Genesis 12:6, 7.

175 Genesis 12:8.

176 Genesis 13:18.

177 See Genesis 22:2, 9 and 2 Chronicles 3:1.

178 Genesis 23:1–20.

179 Genesis 33:18–20.

180 Joshua 24:32.

181 Genesis 28:10–22.

182 See Joshua 14:12–14; 15:13.

183 See 2 Samuel 2:4.

184 Sourced from the State of Palestine Embassy Fact Sheet available at http://www.palestine-australia.com/assets/Uploads/Factsheet-Hebron-AUS24082016.pdf.

185 http://smartraveller.gov.au/Countries/middle-east/Pages/israel_gaza_strip_and_west_bank.aspx.

186 See Genesis 22:1–19.

187 Annexation is the political transition of land from the control of one entity to another. It is also the

incorporation of unclaimed land into a state's sovereignty.

188 The Jordanian *waqf* is an Islamic religious trust that controls and manages the current Islamic edifices on and around the Temple Mount in the Old City of Jerusalem.

189 Ayaan Hirsi Ali is a Somali-born, Dutch-American activist, feminist, author, and former Dutch politician. She founded the AHA Foundation, a nonprofit organization for the defence of women's rights. A former practicing Muslim, Hirsi Ali is an atheist.

190 http://www.jpost.com/Arts-and-Culture/Books/Ayaan-Hirsi-Ali-on-Israel.

191 See Exodus 12:36 that tells us that the Hebrews left Egypt with great wealth after plundering the nation.

192 http://www.aish.com/h/iid/48964091.html.

193 The Anti-Defamation League was founded in 1913 to stop the defamation of the Jewish people and to secure justice and fair treatment to all.

194 Sourced from https://www.adl.org/news/press-releases/adl-global-100-poll.

195 http://www.virtualjerusalem.com/news.php?Itemid=11334.

196 Ibid.

197 Ibid.

198 Ibid.

199 https://karmicreaction.com/2017/01/01/jewish-proverbs/.

200 http://www.chabad.org/library/article_cdo/aid/3074/jewish/28-Teachings.htm.

201 Balad is an Arab political party with four current members in the Knesset.

202 http://www.jpost.com/Diplomacy-and-Politics/Tibi-Nothings-more-praiseworthy-than-martyrdom.

203 The Likud–National Liberal Movement, is a major right-wing political party in Israel. Prime Minister Netanyahu is from Likud.

204 The Joint List was formed in the build-up to the 2015 elections as an alliance of Balad, Hadash, Ta'al and the United Arab List.

205 Arutz Sheva 7 news on 8/3/2017 (http://www.israelnationalnews.com/News/News.aspx/202242)

206 http://www.jpost.com/Arab-Israeli-Conflict/Arab-Israeli-MKs-have-warm-and-productive-meeting-with-terrorists-families-443876

207 http://foreignpolicy.com/2012/04/05/israels-resilient-democracy/.

208 https://en.wikipedia.org/wiki/Ayaan_Hirsi_Ali#Books_.28selected.29

209 The Islamic Waqf is an Islamic religious trust (sometimes called an "Islamic Religious Endowments" organization) best known for controlling and managing the current Islamic edifices on and around the Temple Mount in the Old City of Jerusalem.

210 http://nypost.com/2008/05/04/israels-gift-to-the-world/.

211 God changed Jacob's name to Israel see Genesis 32:28.

212 http://www.jpost.com/Israel-News/Benjamin-Netanyahu/READ-Full-text-of-Netanyahus-speech-to-UN-General-Assembly-468500.

213 Netanyahu served as the Israeli ambassador to the United Nations from 1984 to 1988.

214 Ibid.

215 Ibid.

216 Ibid.

217 Ibid.
218 All rankings that are listed were from the 2013 survey.
219 http://www.theworldfolio.com/interviews/innovative-israel-model-of-resilience/3506/.
220 According to OECD Report in 2012 http://www.haaretz.com/israel-news/israel-ranked-second-most-educated-country-in-the-world-study-shows-1.410415.
221 https://en.wikipedia.org/wiki/Portal:Israel/Did_you_know.
222 Jerusalem Post, Dec 5, 2007, www.jpost.com/Business/./Israel-leads-world-in-per-capita-scientists-and-engineers.
223 https://en.wikipedia.org/wiki/List_of_countries_by_research_and_development_spending.
224 http://www.jpost.com/Israel-News/Benjamin-Netanyahu/READ-Full-text-of-Netanyahus-speech-to-UN-General-Assembly-468500.
225 From Clean-Tech's website: http://www.cleantech.com/indexes/the-global-cleantech-innovation-index/.
226 http://www.businessinsider.com.au/facebook-google-microsoft-israel-rd-2016-10?r=UK&IR=T.
227 Ibid.
228 Ibid.
229 http://timesofindia.indiatimes.com/business/international-business/Google-chief-says-Israeli-tech-second-only-to-Silicon-Valley/articleshow/52753879.cms.
230 http://www.businessinsider.com.au/facebook-google-microsoft-israel-rd-2016-10?r=UK&IR=T.
231 Ibid.
232 *Chutzpah*, the Yiddish word meaning self-confidence and audacity.
233 http://www.businessinsider.com.au/facebook-google-microsoft-israel-rd-2016-10?r=UK&IR=T.
234 https://en.wikipedia.org/wiki/Arms_shipments_from_Czechoslovakia_to_Israel_1947 per centE2 per cent80 per cent9349#cite_note-morris 2008p117-6.
235 Haganah was a Jewish paramilitary organisation in the British Mandate of Palestine, which became the core of the Israel Defence Forces.
236 www.jewishvirtuallibrary.org/jsource/History/1948_War.html.
237 http://www.globalfirepower.com/country-military-strength-detail.asp?country_id=israel.
238 http://www.jpost.com/Israel-News/Israels-air-force-the-best-in-the-world-study-finds-380030.
239 http://www.haaretz.com/israel-news/1.623249.
240 SIPRI is an independent international institute dedicated to research into conflict, armaments, arms control and disarmament.
241 http://books.sipri.org/files/FS/SIPRIFS1512.pdf.
242 War of Attrition involved fighting between Israel and Egypt, Jordan, PLO and their allies from 1967 to 1970.
243 http://www.jpost.com/Israel-News/Benjamin-Netanyahu/READ-Full-text-of-Netanyahus-speech-to-UN-General-Assembly-468500.

244 Ibid.
245 http://www.israel21c.org/israel-in-top-5-happiest-countries-in-the-world/.
246 Ibid.
247 http://www.haaretz.com/israel-news/1.778188.
248 http://www.theworldfolio.com/interviews/innovative-israel-model-of-resilience/3506/.
249 See Exodus 3:8.
250 See Amos 9:13–15.
251 http://www.jewishvirtuallibrary.org/jsource/Quote/TwainJews.html.
252 http://www.jewishvirtuallibrary.org/jsource/History/Arabs_in_Palestine.html.
253 British War cabinet minutes, October 31, 1917.
254 Ibid.
255 http://www.timesofisrael.com/remembering-the-man-who-battled-israels-most-formidable-enemy-the-mosquito/.
256 Beisan is today called Beit She'an, in the Jordan Valley.
257 Israel Jacob Kligler (April 24, 1888–September 23, 1944) was a microbiologist. A Zionist and humanist, he was born in the Austro-Hungarian Empire, educated in the United States, and spent most of his career in Mandatory Palestine, but he died before the creation of the State of Israel. He was one of the first four professors of the Hebrew University and the founder of Department of Hygiene and Bacteriology of the university, which he headed until his death in 1944.
258 http://www.timesofisrael.com/remembering-the-man-who-battled-israels-most-formidable-enemy-the-mosquito/.
259 Ibid.
260 Ibid.
261 A new NASA study finds that the recent drought that began in 1998 in the eastern Mediterranean Levant region, which comprises Cyprus, Israel, Jordan, Lebanon, Palestine, Syria, and Turkey, is likely the worst drought of the past nine centuries. https://www.nasa.gov/feature/goddard/2016/nasa-finds-drought-in-eastern-mediterranean-worst-of-past-900-years.
262 Desalinisation is simple the removal of salt and other dissolved solids from sea water.
263 Water-Gen was named by Fast Company which is a monthly American business that focuses on technology, business, and design as a top Innovative company in 2014.
264 http://www.businessinsider.com.au/water-gen-water-out-of-air-2016-9.
265 http://www.jpost.com/Green-Israel/Water-for-Israel/Limans-in-the-Negev.
266 Cytokinin is a hormone that slows down the aging of leaves in plants.
267 Lonely Planet is the largest travel guide book publisher in the world.
268 http://www.lonelyplanet.com/israel-and-the-palestinian-territories/mediterranean-coast/tel-aviv/introduction.
269 http://www.jewishvirtuallibrary.org/agriculturally-coping-with-population-growth.
270 http://www.jpost.com/National-News/Israeli-cows-outperform-their-foreign-counterparts.

271 Jeremiah 31:9–12.
272 http://www.israel21c.org/israeli-olive-oil-comes-of-age/.
273 http://www.indexmundi.com/agriculture/?country=il&commodity=olive-oil&graph=production; http://www.indexmundi.com/agriculture/?country=il&commodity=olive-oil&graph=domestic-consumption.
274 http://www.haaretz.com/israel-news/business/uprooting-israel-s-olive-industry-1.464471.
275 The garagistes refers to a group of winemakers that produce "garage wine." Most "garage wineries" produce small lots of limited production wines.
276 http://winesisrael.com/en/3713/harvest-2016/.
277 http://www.haaretz.com/science-and-health/1.799726.
278 http://www.jpost.com/Business-and-Innovation/Health-and-Science/Israeli-Harvard-researchers-to-improve-insulin-management-for-type-1-diabetics-490238.
279 http://www.tevapharm.com/our_products/generic_products/.
280 Copaxone (glatiramer acetate) is a combination of four amino acids (proteins) used to treat multiple sclerosis (MS) and to prevent relapse of MS. Copaxone will not cure MS, but it can make relapses occur less often.
281 https://www.reuters.com/article/teva-pharm-ind-results-idUSL5N10A3VA20150730
282 https://www.israel21c.org/israel-facts/technology/.
283 https://www.israel21c.org/israelis-build-worlds-first-eye-free-smartphone/.
284 https://www.israel21c.org/storedot-wows-world-with-30-second-phone-charger/.
285 http://www.charismanews.com/opinion/standing-with-israel/61028-israel-a-modern-day-miracle.
286 The Washington Institute for Near East Policy was founded in 1985, for the advancement of a balanced and realistic understanding of American interests in the Middle East and to promote the policies that secure them.
287 http://www.jpost.com/Opinion/Why-America-needs-Israel-400492.
288 http://www.jpost.com/Israel-News/Politics-And-Diplomacy/Military-exports-rise-to-65-billion-485574.
289 Sourced from https://www.sipri.org/sites/default/files/Trends-in-international-arms-transfers-2016.pdf.
290 http://www.jpost.com/Israel-News/Politics-And-Diplomacy/Military-exports-rise-to-65-billion-485574.
291 MASHAV is the Hebrew acronym for Israel's Agency for International Development Cooperation.
292 http://www.jpost.com/Business-and-Innovation/Tech/Tell-us-how-you-made-Israel-470231.
293 http://mfa.gov.il/MFA/mashav/AboutMASHAV/Pages/Background.aspx.
294 http://www.jpost.com/Business-and-Innovation/Environment/Bhutanese-minister-Diplomatic-relations-with-Israel-are-possible-466889.
295 USAID, United States Agency for International Development, is the US agency with the primarily responsibility for administering civilian foreign aid.
296 http://cnpublications.net/2016/10/22/israel-farms-the-world/.
297 GIZ German International Development Corporation.

298 http://www.timesofisrael.com/the-israei-guest-thats-welcome-around-the-world/.
299 http://www.jpost.com/Business-and-Innovation/Tech/Tell-us-how-you-made-Israel-470231.
300 IFAD, the International Fund for Agricultural Development, is an international financial institution and a specialised agency of the United Nations dedicated to eradicating poverty and hunger in rural areas of developing countries.
301 http://embassies.gov.il/yaounde/NewsAndEvents/Pages/MASHAV-and-PEA-Jeunes-sign-MoU.aspx.
302 http://cnpublications.net/2016/10/22/israel-farms-the-world/.
303 Ibid.
304 12 Chemists, 11 Physicists 11 Medicine and Physiology, 11 Economists and 5 in various fields of literature.
305 Sourced from https://en.wikipedia.org/wiki/List_of_Jewish_Nobel_laureates.
306 https://newrepublic.com/article/115339/richard-dawkins-interview-archbishop-atheism.
307 The Kyoto Prize is an international award to honor those who have contributed significantly to the scientific, cultural, and spiritual betterment of mankind.
308 The prize is awarded in Israel by the Wolf Foundation, founded by Dr Ricardo Wolf, a German-born inventor and former Cuban ambassador to Israel. It is awarded in six fields: agriculture, chemistry, mathematics, medicine, physics, and an arts prize that rotates between architecture, music, painting, and sculpture.
309 The National Medal of Science is an honour bestowed by the president of the United States to individuals in science and engineering who have made important contributions to the advancement of knowledge in the fields of behavioral and social sciences, biology, chemistry, engineering, mathematics and physics.
310 The Grande Médaille of the French Academy of Sciences, established in 1997, is awarded annually to a researcher who has contributed decisively to the development of science.
311 https://www.thoughtco.com/most-influential-scientists-in-20th-century-1779904.
312 http://content.time.com/time/magazine/article/0,9171,993017,00.html.
313 The photoelectric effect is the emission of electrons or other free carriers when light is shone onto a material. Electrons emitted in this manner can be called photo electrons.
314 A system of psychological theory and therapy which aims to treat mental disorders by investigating the interaction of conscious and unconscious elements in the mind and bringing repressed fears and conflicts into the conscious mind by techniques such as dream interpretation and free association.
315 Quantum mechanics is the science that deals with the behaviour of matter and light on the atomic and subatomic level.
316 The Manhattan Project was a research and development undertaking during World War II that produced the first nuclear weapons.
317 http://www.adherents.com/people/100_scientists.html. In this survey, Einstein ranked 2nd behind Isaac Newton, Bohr was 3rd and Freud 6th.
318 http://www.jta.org/2016/03/02/news-opinion/united-states/mark-zuckerberg-is-the-worlds-richest-jew-according-to-forbes-billionaire-list.
319 Nixon's 1972 visit to the People's Republic of China was an important step in formally normalizing

relations between the United States and China. It marked the first time a U.S. president had visited the People's Republic of China ending 25 years of separation between the two sides.

320 The Moscow Summit of May 1972 between Nixon and Leonid Brezhnev featured the signing of the Anti-Ballistic Missile (ABM) Treaty, the first Strategic Arms Limitation Treaty (SALT I). The summit is considered one of the hallmarks of the détente at the time between the two Cold War antagonists.

321 *Oxford Treasury of Sayings and Quotations* (Oxord Univeristy Press, 2011), 382.

322 See Revelation 21:9–22:5.

323 Romans 9:33.

324 Acts 4:11.

325 Romans 9:33.

326 See chapter 3.

327 πίπτω piptō, to fall under judgment, came under condemnation.

328 παράπτωμα, paraptōma, a side-slip a trespass a deviation from truth.

329 Gentiles is a Biblical term for are all non-Jews.

330 See Romans 9:30–31.

331 Romans 9:27.

332 See 2 Corinthians 3:15.

333 See Acts 2:36 and 4:10.

334 See Acts 2:23 and 1 Peter 1:19–20.

335 The four quarters are Jewish, Muslim, Christian and Armenian. The Armineans consider their quarter Christian. The three Christian patriarchates of Jerusalem and the government of Armenia have publicly expressed their opposition to any political division of the Arminean and Christian quarters.

336 Ben means son of. Messiah the son of Joseph and Messiah the son of David.

337 For a fuller explanation of this Jewish belief, see http://www.hebrew4christians.com/Articles/Mashiach_ben_Yosef/mashiach_ben_yosef.html.

338 See Revelation 5:5.

339 The Tanakh is an acronym of the first Hebrew letter of each of the three traditional subdivisions of the Jewish Bible. Torah, the first five books called the law, the Nevi'im called "the prophets" and the Ketuvim called "the writings."

340 Hebrew, like most Middle Eastern languages are read from right to left.

341 See Revelation 1:8, 11 Alpha and Omega are the first and the last letters of the Greek alphabet.

342 See John 1:1 and 1:14.

343 See Matthew 26:28.

344 See chapter 2.

345 See Deuteronomy 28:1–14.

346 See Romans 10:4.

347 See Deuteronomy 28:64–6.

348 See 2 Corinthians 3:7; Hebrew 8:7, 8.

349 http://www.slate.com/blogs/the_slatest/2014/11/09/iran_s_khamenei_israel_must_be_annihilated.html.

350 Ali Shirazi is a senior Iranian cleric who is Supreme Leader Ayatollah Ali Khamenei's representative to

the Islamic Revolutionary Guards Corps-Quds Force (IRGC-QF). He holds the clerical ranking of Hojatoleslam, which is the rank below Ayatollah.

351 http://www.israelnationalnews.com/Articles/Article.aspx/14336.

352 Ibid.

353 Ibid.

354 Sahih Muslim Book 041, Hadith Number 6985.

355 See Matthew 24:21–22.

356 See 1 Corinthians 16:22.

357 See Matthew 21:9.

358 See Luke 23:13–25.

359 *Baruch ha-ba b'shem Adonai*: "Blessed is He who comes in the name of the Lord!"

www.ingramcontent.com/pod-product-compliance
Lightning Source LLC
Chambersburg PA
CBHW052037070526
44584CB00016B/2076